Padma Bharatis

Padma Bharatis

Ordinary Indians, Extraordinary Triumphs

Curated by
Jay Jina

To D.V. Sridharan ji, whose Good News India stories inspired this work

कर्मण्येवाधिकारस्ते मा फलेषु कदाचन ।
मा कर्मफलहेतुर्भूर्मा ते सङ्गोऽस्त्वकर्मणि ॥ २-४७॥

karmaṇy-evādhikāras te mā phaleṣu kadācana.
mā karma-phala-hetur bhūr mā te saṅgo 'stvakarmaṇi

Since you are entitled only to the performance of action but never to the fruits thereof, you should neither desire rewards of action nor be drawn to inaction.
Bhagavad Gita 2:47

Contents

A Note from the Curator

India, that is, Bharat, embodies diversity to a degree that few other places can match. Here, one finds a true *chitraayana*, a colourful life force peopled by incredible souls whose lives exude a vibrant *maanyata* and *maryaada* – respect and dignity – where diversity itself is crafted by a seemingly timeless unity in multiplexity.

This is a culture of cultures bonded by a long and rich tradition of creativity and ingenuity. Every day, amazing results of human endeavour are visible in many fields of daily life, with ordinary people accomplishing extraordinary feats.

Inspired by D.V. Sridharan's book, *Good News India: Ordinary Indians, Extraordinary Triumphs* (Bloomsbury, 2021), we at INDICA wondered what could be a better way to acknowledge and celebrate the amazing and inspiring journeys of just a few of these ordinary yet extraordinary folk than via an anthology? This book, comprising a dozen essays, is the result.

It is remarkable that, over recent years, public recognition of the extraordinary accomplishments of ordinary Indians has witnessed a paradigm shift. The make-up of Padma awardees reflects this shift: more than ever before, the lists are decorated by ordinary, previously unknown people who represent the true diversity of India. Every one of them has a rich and compelling story to share. Regardless of social status, geographical location, economic circumstances, station in life, or access to formal education, it is the extraordinary work and achievements of the subjects that stand out. Indeed, recalling Mark Twain's thoughts on the matter, it is apt to say that among our stories of triumph are several whose subjects never let the absence of formal schooling interfere with their education.

Prominent in these stories are tales in which steely determination and single-minded focus overcome huge obstacles and achieve tangible results that improve lives and build stronger communities. Here are women and men who are not simply unafraid to embrace and deliver sustainable change but who also maintain trust in traditions, culture and crafts, and confidently use experiential knowledge that has been passed down over generations.

The subjects are earthy, raw, real, and often rustic or small-town people, each inspired by core values that stem from a civilisation that is finding its bearings while squarely dealing with the challenges on the road to a sustainable, aspirational future. In many ways, their stories are truly universal and will resonate with people everywhere, even for those who may see India as strange and mysterious.

I am grateful to Shri Hari Kiran Vadlamani, founder of INDICA, for conceiving this project and allowing me to curate and edit this anthology in what has been an incredible journey. Hari Kiran continues to inspire and empower so many, and I feel truly blessed and privileged to work on this anthology.

I have been supported by the consulting team comprising Hari, Ramesh Rao, D.V. Sridharan, and Dimple Kaul. It is fair to say that each member of the consulting team has contributed immensely to the spirit that is embodied in the anthology.

Aside from supporting me with the onerous task of final editing of the essays, Ramesh has offered guidance and shared his invaluable insights and deep knowledge of the Indian social landscape at each stage.

DV, as we fondly call D.V. Sridharan, always a font of wisdom and a joy to interact with, provided an author's style guide in the spirit of his book *Good News India*. He unhesitatingly answered questions and offered advice when called upon, and I am grateful that even recovering from major surgery did not impede his boundless enthusiasm.

Dimple Kaul, thank you for sharing your valuable experience from your work on *Good News India*, which helped in setting the course for this project.

A deep debt of gratitude is also due to Michael Thorn, whose keen eye and meticulous proofreading have helped in making the overall work what it is.

A work of this type would not have been possible without the passionate support and publishing expertise of Praveen Tiwari at BluOne Ink. INDICA is grateful of the confidence he has shown for this project.

Of course, this anthology relies entirely upon contributions. We are fortunate to have garnered an amazingly enthusiastic and talented cross-section of authors who have been a delight to work with. Whether new or seasoned in narrative writing, each of our authors has taken on the challenge to present their chosen subject as driven, visionary, practical, pragmatic and, above all, human. Each of their choices is an exemplar of courage in the face of adversity and refusal to be deterred in pursuit of their goals.

It has been a joy to mentor those authors who are fairly new to this genre of writing and pleasing to note that many have expressed that exchanging ideas as each essay went through multiple iterative stages, has proved to be an enriching experience.

It is also noteworthy that two of the contributions are from teenagers, both of whom have produced pieces that bely their tender years, not least because the challenges were especially great, since both are far from India, being based in USA.

I would like to thank my friend Prashanth Prabhu of Bengaluru and his college friend Sarfraz Hassim of PA College, Mangaluru, who serendipitously came to the rescue and helped one of our teenage authors make contact with his chosen subject, Harekala Hajjaba. In this regard, thanks are also due to Aparna Sridhar who, besides being a contributor to this anthology, also offered her support with translation for this story.

I am grateful to all authors, and especially the experienced ones for putting up with what may have sometimes felt like exacting demands. Each of them generously shared their knowledge and experience with me, responded positively and iterated their narratives to get their final manuscripts aligned to achieve the spirit and substance of the style guide.

All that said, individuals' time constraints, personal circumstances and conflicts with other priorities meant that a few of the original expressions of interest to submit a story did not come to fruition, and it is hoped that these equally interesting and inspiring stories shall be covered in a future edition of a similar anthology.

It is hoped that the result is a compelling set of stories of triumph that readers will find informative so that they stimulate self-reflection; humane so that they project the best of not just *maryaada* and *maanyata* but also *mamta* and *shakti* – a nurturing, empowering love; educative, reaffirming confidence and optimism about being Indian;

and also inspiring and capable of motivating even a small number towards action.

It seems apposite that each of our subjects is a Padma awardee, for the Padma is truly honoured to have been bestowed on these women and men.

Jay Jina
Director, Chitraayana
INDICA

Preface: The Eternal Machine

Looking back, the period between 1943, the year of Britain-engineered food famine in Bengal, and the year 2000 – also called Y2K, which unleashed India's digital prowess – may indeed be deemed a period of doom and gloom in Indian history.

News of food shortages, starvation-driven deaths, political instability, rising poverty, rampant corruption, and unstable borders arrived daily, which induced despondency and added to the glee of global media reporting on India.

There was indeed genuine bad news the press could not have ignored, but surely there was some good too happening at large?

Asking that question may have helped me pioneer a genre of reporting nothing but the good news.

My justification for this was that there were enough media outlets to front page the bad news, but hardly any featuring what good there indeed was.

I noticed some few-line snippets of good work appeared occasionally at the bottom of the inner pages of the big newspapers. After collecting a few, I took to the road to authenticate my leads.

The instant success of goodnewsindia.com (GNI) convinced me there was a hunger at large for genuine good news. Many readers wrote in suggesting leads I could consider writing on.

Conversely, there was also evidence that readers will intuitively resist reports however well couched in 'fact', if the derived conclusions were preposterous.

Let me explain with an example of what a preposterous story may be like.

I spent my 1960s in the merchant marine. During those times, many shiploads of grains from Australia, New Zealand, and the Americas were transported to India as aid-gift. With barely concealed condescension I have had it whispered to me by cargo loaders in overseas harbours, how their country was happy to feed 'the starving millions of India'. Concealing my humiliation was not easy.

It was also the time when a series of depressing books and articles on the apparent hopelessness of India began to appear – among them, V.S. Naipaul's *An Area of Darkness* and Nirad Chaudhury's *The Continent of Circe.*

Famine, 1975! America's Decision: Who Will Survive?, a book by William Paddock and Paul Paddock published in 1967, prophesied the death of India within a decade. The authors argued thus: per the oracle of Malthus, by 1975 world population will have grown beyond maintainability, and all the food that can possibly be grown in the world cannot save the dying millions; therefore, the two most hopeless countries in the authors' list – India and Egypt – should be allowed to perish, so that the rest of the world may live.

And so it was that, into an India enveloped in such dismissive global contempt that GNI – Good News India – was born, asserting itself in its masthead thus: 'News from India: of positive action, steely endeavour and quiet triumphs – news that is little known.'

I set for myself a few rules:

1. Reporting good news calls for greater responsibility than posting fake or biased.

2. No coverage of politics, cinema or cricket.
3. All stories should be written consequent upon personal interviews.
4. The real hero doesn't emerge until the interviewer has discovered the 'aha moment' that transformed the hero.

Travels to many parts of the country to interview my leads revealed a vastness where a sense of eternity reigned. I began to visualise it in many metaphors.

I imagined India as a giant pyramid whose bottom third ensures its stability and permanence. I found the bottom third.

There was a comfort in knowing the bottom third has the most people and that they were truly the ones investing in India.

I imagined permanence as a perpetual machine akin to a giant flywheel kept in motion by billions of Bharatiyas of yore and of the morrow. I persuaded myself that the perpetual machine is indeed what is commonly known to us as sanatana dharma.

All machines are systems that function beneficially only when a set of rules are adhered to.

These I believed to be the four laws of human life – namely, *artha, kama,* dharma, and *moksha* – which I took to be representing reward, happiness, discipline, and fulfilment. It follows that any work is good that contributes to the perpetuity and prosperity of the whole.

After some years of publishing GNI, I realised reporting or reading good news alone doesn't amount to good work. At best, such stories may inspire one to good work.

I searched for and bought 20 acres of land that had been abandoned for being devoid of water and topsoil. Undertaking to restore it to productive health, using water harvesting and stopping soil erosion, seemed like it could amount to my little push to the giant wheel of my imagination.

Thus, what had begun as a search for good news had found me my own modest mission.

In 2008, I posted my last story in GNI and, with that, I ceased updating the site and turned entirely to my restoration work to regenerate the land I had acquired.

I expected GNI to fade away. It did not. Over the years, a core of the 6,000 readers on my mailing list kept writing to wish I would resume reporting and writing. But I had moved on, content that the power of good work by little-known Indians of whom I had written had had some impact on many of my readers.

Suddenly one morning in 2017, I read in the newspapers that Girish Bharadwaj was to be awarded a Padma Shri. I recalled the time 15 years earlier when I had visited him to discuss his work building bridges to flooded and isolated villages so that they could remain connected with the mainland. Two years later, in 2019, another of my GNI heroes, Saalumarada Thimmakka, who I had front-paged in 2002, was also awarded the Padma Shri.

I was delighted that in both cases, the official announcement had used photos taken by me for my stories.

It was clear: a big shift had occurred in New Delhi.

An informally educated village boy from Gujarat had assumed office as Prime Minister in 2014. Narendra Damodardas Modi knew who nurtures and strengthens this land. They are mostly those in the bottom third of the pyramid. They keep the perpetual machine in motion. In their well-being and active involvement in keeping the wheels moving lay the permanence and prosperity of this ancient land.

Modi began to clean Delhi of the coterie which had occupied sprawling government bungalows, manipulated the system to have its choices appointed as ministers and public servants, influenced the selection of Padma awardees, siphoned bank treasuries, brokered arms deals, facilitated engineered demographic change, and more besides ... it was a Crony Collective that was in power when Modi took over.

Even while this cleaning up was on, Modi's office began to routinely scan the many good works underway across the country and bring them to his notice.

Through his frequent televised conversations called *Mann ki Baat*, he shares stories of little-known Indians adding value to Bharat.

Today, Indic Academy's decision to publish a series on the good work by Padma awardees takes the propagation of authentic good news to another level. Each article enlarges the story beyond the award brief and draws the reader to reflect on what her contribution could be to this land.

I wish the series all success.

D.V. Sridharan
Chennai, India
17 April 2024

1

'Beej Mata': The Seed Mother

Madhavi Girish Kunte

A long, winding journey through difficult terrain brings us to Poperewadi, a tiny village in the Kombhalne district of Ahmednagar taluka (a subdivision of a district), about 200 km from Pune. Here lives a grandma, fondly known as '*Beej Mata*' (the Seed Mother) of India, Rahibai Popere. You will find her on a hilltop, surrounded by lush green pasture, toiling away in her small field, day in and day out. To an untrained eye, the field may seem deceptively small, but contrary to that perception her field is a goldmine of indigenous seed varieties.

It had rained the previous night. The sweet smell of damp soil was in the air and the farm appeared clean and fresh, as it always does after rains. To my left, the field was overflowing with guava, papaya, dahlia, marigold, and a variety of leafy green vegetables. To the right of the walkway, across the field, sat a small building complex with rooms arranged in a square, with an open centre. Here, too, guava trees laden with small fruit stood tall in the company of papaya, creating a small private garden set off from the main farm. Within this complex was space for living quarters, along with a meeting room and a couple of guest rooms.

I found her seated in the meeting room with a group of perhaps a dozen farmers who had come to visit her from near and far. They were making seed packages for distribution among other farmers from their respective areas. They packed hundreds of seeds in crates and loaded them onto motorcycles, then bade us a hearty farewell, making their way back down the mountain track that I had just come up.

Before I can turn to greet her again and introduce myself properly, she is already sweeping the room. I offer to help but, continuing with her task, she says, 'I want to welcome my guests in a clean room.' I want to tell her that her meeting room in the middle of a farm is much cleaner than many places in the cities!

When I compliment her on the greenery and the thriving saplings on her farm, she simply replies that I am fortunate to be visiting during the rainy season. During the rest of the year, the land in and around the farm is mostly dry. When I point to the small lake nearby, she says that the water there is for cattle, goats and sheep to sustain them during the dry months, and even farmers are not allowed to divert water for farming activities.

Since Rahibai's farm is located in the upper reaches among the hills, she really is dependent on the rains to water her plants.

Before we settle down to talk at length about her work and achievements, Rahibai offers a tour of her farm. She shows me the different varieties of vegetables and pulses that she cultivates. Making our way among the well laid-out plants, I notice some clear pugmarks, which the previous night's rains have caused to be very clearly imprinted on the wet earth. I instinctively look around for a huge, striped cat, but by then my host has moved far ahead of me, deeper into the farm, mildly complaining about how difficult it is to protect the cattle from tigers and even an elusive leopard.

Rahibai uses only organic cow dung as manure for the soil. When I ask how she combats insects and pests without chemical fertiliser, pesticides and sprays, she talks about herbal pesticides. She tells me how women in her household prepare an herbal compound from the leaves of neem, custard apple or sitaphal and other trees. Each batch takes two weeks to prepare, and it is so effective that the crop yields are as good as on farms using chemical pesticides. Rahibai explains that the main difference is not between the quantities of yield, but the quality of the crop and that of the land. Once chemicals are used, the land becomes dependant on these external sources and loses its natural tendency to renew itself and replenish its nutrients; whereas the soil treated with organic manure is not only enriched in nutrients but also offers shelter to farmers' friends, such as earthworms, that help sustain the land.

Rahibai farms with the sole intent of harvesting seeds while subsisting on the other produce grown. The green leafy vegetables and much of the fruit are sufficient for the family's consumption and are not produced for market.

Born into a poor farmer's family in 1964, Rahibai is used to a harsh life, where a full day's hard work is needed to provide enough for each day's meals and shelter. As the fourth daughter in the household, she often had to tend to her younger siblings. Her youngest sister was nine months old when their mother passed away. The family used to farm during the rainy season and the rest of the year they all worked as casual labourers in nearby sugar mills or as hired help on larger, commercial farms where resources such as irrigation facilities made it possible to cultivate crops all year around.

Rahibai mentions that her father was the one person who truly motivated her and really touched her life. Although poor and uneducated, he had nurtured his seven daughters with good values and striven to impart life lessons to all of them.

Rahibai swears by her father's teachings and feels indebted to him in many ways. Even today, she continues to live by the teachings imparted by a simple, unassuming, rustic son of the soil. She does not shy away from quoting his words again and again, stressing how important they remain and the strength and motivation that still flow from them.

'*Garibi ali tar laju nahi ani shrimanti ali tar maaju nahi*' (Do not be ashamed of poverty, and do not be proud of your wealth).

'*Changlya kama madhey marun nighaycha pan sarun nighaycha nahi*' (Never give up on a good deed even if you have to sacrifice your life).

Married into a typical traditional family of poor farmers at the tender age of twelve, life did not get any easier for Rahibai. She lived the better part of the first twenty-two years of married life in a cow-shed and gave birth to her children amidst the cattle. Barely a few hours after childbirth, she would get up and take charge of household chores and, not too long after, be out and about tending to the farm with her days-old infant strapped on her back.

The age of hybrids had begun and everyone around her was cultivating hybrid crop varieties sustained by increased usage of chemical fertilisers and pesticides. Rahibai's family followed suit: the yield increased, but so did the cost of production. The consumption of produce laced with chemical fertilisers, however, took a heavy toll on family health. There was a constant influx of previously unknown illnesses in the home and the cost of medical expenses mounted up.

With moist eyes, Rahibai recalls the difficult days when she had to sell jewellery and cattle to meet medical expenses. One time, when her grandson was admitted into hospital and had to stay there for over a month, the family had to mortgage a part of their farm to pay the bills.

Following one such visit to the hospital, while returning home, Rahibai sat down under a tree, feeling dejected and defeated. She wondered what had gone wrong.

Earlier, the family did not suffer from such frequent illnesses. Young women would give birth to healthy babies and get back to work in no time. What had happened to their inner strength? They no longer seemed as healthy and there was so much more dependence on medication.

She realised that this vicious cycle had set in when they had switched to using chemicals. It seemed that this had not only caused illnesses, but over time, the soil also was losing its nutrients and regenerative capacity as it became more dependent on external chemical sources of nutrition just to maintain fertility.

Rahibai decided that enough was enough. She urged everyone in her family to give up on hybrid varieties and chemical fertilisers, pesticides, and insecticides. In doing this, she was going against the tide and naturally faced much resistance. She candidly recalls her own personal non-cooperation movement at home, when, to get her point across, she withdrew from contributing to the family's activities and even sat out of all daily happenings. She was determined to fight for a worthy cause and she felt that this was her own *Satyagraha* to win over those close to her on the home front.

Gradually, her perseverance paid off and members of the family decided to support her ideas of growing indigenous varieties on their farm. Chemical fertilisers were replaced with organic cow dung manure. This was no sudden change: the family took slow and measured steps to wean the soil off chemicals.

Since the source of irrigation for Rahibai's land on the hilltop is predominantly the rain, the harvest is limited to what grows during the rainy season. Outside of the planting and harvesting months, just as previous generations had done, the family would take up odd jobs to maintain a steady income for the household. Instead of doing this in the off-season, Rahibai began preparing saplings of indigenous varieties, which she continues doing to this day. She began by giving away these saplings as gifts to her neighbours and to women who lived in the locality whenever she met them at cultural gatherings. Slowly and steadily, Rahibai's innovative ideas caught on with people in her neighbourhood, but that did not immediately lead to them giving up the use of chemical and hybrid crops. Progress was slow – it took her a lot of time and effort to achieve the results that Rahibai desired from her work.

While some neighbours and acquaintances applauded her initiative and pointed out that she was doing a thankless job, Rahibai had to brave much scepticism and many jibes. Yet she persisted in her goals.

As her work came to be recognised, Rahibai received support from the tribal development project of General Mills, implemented by BAIF Development Research Organisation (formerly registered as Bharatiya Agro Industries Foundation). Initially, they provided various perennial saplings such as mango, sapodilla custard apple, papaya, lemon, moringa, *Sesbania grandiflora*, and fig, which helped her develop her kitchen garden. They also offered training on plantation techniques and aftercare.

The breakthrough in Rahibai's journey came when the regional head of BAIF, Jitin Sathe, chanced upon her vast collection of indigenous seeds. She showed Sathe her collection, each variety carefully stored in the traditional manner within ash inside earthen pots. Rahibai claimed that the shelf life for planting these seeds was three years and that they would remain suitable for consumption even after being stored for more than five years. Sathe took the seed samples with him, had them tested in the laboratory and found that they were all indigenous varieties just as Rahibai had claimed. The scientist realised that, in fact, Rahibai had in her collection 48 varieties of the indigenous food crop seeds as well as other seeds of medicinal plants only found in the jungle that few farmers ever bothered to cultivate. Despite lacking even a rudimentary formal education, Rahibai was able to give Sathe detailed information on each variety and made him realise that she was a font of knowledge and her farm a treasure trove of rare varieties of both edible and medicinal plants.

Since then, BAIF has continued to support Rahibai's ideas and promote her work by transferring knowledge of techniques such as mulching, making her knowledge better-known to the scientific community and promoting her on various media platforms. A key instance of this was when a leading Marathi daily, *Sakal,* published in Pune, wrote a well-received feature article about Rahibai's pioneering work, making it more widely known for the first time.

Rahibai runs exhibitions, workshops, symposiums, and farmer-training programmes organised at both state and national levels to promote knowledge and propagation of indigenous varieties. BAIF continues to be a steadfast source of support for Rahibai and extends help in the organising of such events and provides assistance with travel plans.

Impressed by her efforts towards conservation of indigenous plants, agriculture experts at BAIF added Rahibai's district, Kombhalne, to the Maharashtra Gene

Bank Project when it was rolled out in the area. A seed bank of indigenous seeds was established in a small room in Rahibai's home and inaugurated in 2016 by Girish Sohani, then president of BAIF. Rahibai has continued to leverage the seed bank to propagate and promote the use of indigenous seeds.

The village seed bank now holds 116 indigenous varieties of 54 crops, which include 20 varieties of beans and over 30 diverse varieties of rice paddy, finger millet (*ragi* or *nagli*), and barnyard millet (*varai*), as well as various oil seeds and vegetables. All these varieties have low moisture requirements, and some are able to thrive with little to no moisture, making them suitable for cultivation in areas with minimal rainfall and for growing and harvesting outside the traditional farming season.

Rahibai considers the black fertile soil to be her mother. She feels that 'if we maintain our mother's health, she will nurture us in return. In order to be strong, we should pay attention to building the strength of our soil.' She strongly believes that farmers are responsible not just for the land but also for the health of the nation, believing that if they are slack in their work, society and the nation suffer. She puts it strongly into words saying, 'Taking the chemical route in the quest for better yields is equivalent to growing poison.'

Support from BAIF and interviews with journalists was soon followed with notable colleges and universities making organised field trips to Rahibai's farm, which led to the farming community also noticing her work. As Rahibai's reach spread and her popularity soared, support for her ideas and methods began to grow on the home front as well. Her local farmer neighbours and friends were now keenly listening to her advice and showing greater willingness to change their approach.

Rahibai's practice of gifting saplings of indigenous plants to rural women within her locality during social gatherings like *Haldi Kumkum* ceremonies became hugely popular, and soon some of the small social gatherings transformed into larger self-help groups of motivated women. These self-help groups in the Akole taluka played an important role in popularising and giving momentum to the initiative. Rahibai helped in establishing Kalsubai Parisar Biyane Samvardhan Samajik Sanstha – the Kalsubai Area Seed Conservation Social Organisation – specialising in the protection and propagation of indigenous food and medicinal plant varieties. By virtue of this initiative, Rahibai has trained 3,500 women farmers through additional self-help groups like the Mahila Bachat Gat.

Today, indigenous varieties continue to gain popularity all over Maharashtra. Rahibai's aim is to take this initiative forward and she has ambitious plans for growth to a national level, with seed banks being set up all over the country so that local farmers in other states can collect, distribute and help cultivate more indigenous varieties and thus preserve plant diversity in India. Her vision is for every village to have their own Rahibai and a local seed bank. In her words, 'It is a precious treasure of nature that needs to be preserved for all future generations.'

Rahibai's long endeavours with this enterprise led eminent scientist and Director General of the Council of Scientific and Industrial Research (CSIR), Dr Raghunath Mashelkar, to give her the honorific name Beej Mata, the mother of seeds. Since then, Rahibai came to be popularly known as Beej Mata in Maharashtra.

Along the way, Rahibai has had numerous awards and accolades bestowed on her by various institutions, private enterprises and media companies, while her work has been recognised and awarded by both the state and the national government.

Although these achievements have brought Rahibai national recognition, as well as name and fame globally, she believes firmly that, for real impact, the journey she began all those years ago must go further. Even after receiving the Padma Shri from President Ram Nath Kovind in 2020, she remains passionate about her work in her fields, steadfastly detached from personal ambition, and solely dedicated to social welfare.

Rahibai's status as a media and public figure has hardly affected her lifestyle: her daily work pattern and quality of life remain the same as they have been for half a century. She and her family still toil hard in their fields, making an honourable living. During the off-season, many of them still go out in search of work elsewhere. As for the seeds, Rahibai does not charge much for them: a small packet of her hard labour and dedication costs only 30 rupees. And yet there have been unscrupulous visitors from 'agricultural institutions' who have taken advantage of her simplicity. She once received a mere 750 rupees for a rare seed variety that was worth 5,000 rupees in the market.

Her only regret in life is that she never had the opportunity for a formal education. She feels that this would have enabled her to express herself better and be more informed about the world. She recalls, with nostalgia, the village school of her childhood. It was a small gathering of pupils, mostly boys, from the neighbouring villages, seated under a tree in the temple premises, being taken through basic literacy. Even though her poor family background did not allow her to be a part of that group in childhood, today she is welcomed into colleges and universities where, despite not having a formal education, she imparts her extensive, field-acquired experience and deep knowledge to eager students.

Even after all the difficulties she has had to face, Rahibai remains positive about life, offering a warm welcome and embracing anyone visiting her home with open arms and a pleasant smile. The pace and grace with which she guides her guests through her farm defy her age. The cucumbers, beans, lemons, and the many varieties of green leafy vegetables are a testament to the sheer hard work and dedication that Rahibai puts into her endeavours.

As I take her leave, the bright red dahlia adorning her front porch fails to compete with her bright smile. While bidding farewell, Rahibai hands me a few cucumbers and some seed packets urging me to taste the sweetness of the gourds and not to forget to plant the seeds. While handing me these parting gifts, she also shared a few more uses of these seeds, telling me that she makes *rakhis* and *rangoli* out of them. She reminded me of Diwali, which was still three months away, as she also murmured something about making small *diyas* from these very seeds especially for the occasion.

Rahibai's field-based, hands-on research methodology and step-by-step progress towards the fruition of her dream is an inspiration and motivation to Indian women who have the aptitude and will to succeed. No circumstance or environment ought to be a barrier in the pursuit of noble dreams.

It is heart-warming to be close to and witness the work and manner of a supposedly untutored person (even one who would be considered illiterate by conventional measures) rise to such great heights, through not just courage, perseverance and willpower but a keen and practically oriented intellect.

Rahibai, like millions around the world just like her, works hard for her living and is able to hold her head high with dignity. Here is a woman of substance – one who thinks, follows up on her ideas and strives to contribute to society even at those times when her own needs remain neglected.

2

The Hospital That Subhasini Mistry Built

Santhini Govindan

The word 'superhero' conjures up an image of a strong, god-like figure with wings or a wand that can create magic. However, sometimes superheroes are just ordinary people with humble beginnings who achieve phenomenal things in a seemingly magical way through their extraordinary willpower and effort. Subhasini Mistry is one such person, but her path to success in fulfilling a unique dream was strewn with many hurdles.

Subhasini Mistry's life got off to a rocky start over 75 years ago, in Kulwa, a small village in West Bengal. She was born into a poor farming family of fourteen children and when just twelve years old was married off to an agricultural daily wage labourer called Sadhan Chandra Mistry who lived in the nearby village of Hanspukur. Sadhan earned a meagre amount every month, and Subhasini had to struggle hard to maintain the household doing daily chores, cooking, and tending to her four children.

One day, in 1971, Sadhan fell ill with acute diarrhoea, and Subhasini took him to the government district hospital in Tollygunge, where poor people were supposed to get free medical attention. But to Subhasini's dismay and despair, the nurses and doctors at the hospital paid no attention to Sadhan's deteriorating condition. Being penniless and lacking influential connections that could have got him the help he so desperately needed, sadly, but unsurprisingly, Sadhan ended up dying from what should have been an entirely curable condition. In one sudden, very unfortunate stroke, Subhasini became a young widow with four children to care for. She was further handicapped by being illiterate, unable to tell the time or count money. At that time, her oldest child was eight years old, and the youngest one was not yet two.

Devastated by this unexpected blow, the young Subhasini, in the midst of her shock and sorrow, knew that it was a lack of timely medical attention that had led to her husband being snatched away so suddenly and unfairly. However, rather than be defeated by her situation, she decided then and there that she would not let anyone else face the misery that she had undergone. She vowed that she would, somehow, build a hospital where poor people would not be dismissed for being poor but be offered quality medical care in time of need. She believed with all her heart that families in poverty should not have to suffer the loss of a breadwinner simply for the want of basic medical care. Subhasini made this emotional pledge when she was in the depths of despair. It would hardly have been surprising if the promise she had made to herself had been forgotten as she struggled to get on with her life, and cope with numerous everyday battles for survival.

But Subhasini was made of sterner stuff. Since her only skill was doing housework, she began working as a maid in five different homes to earn just enough to feed her family. She worked hard, toiling for long hours, turning her hand to all manner of household chores like cooking, sweeping, mopping floors, and washing. It was backbreaking drudgery, and though Subhasini did it stoically while also caring for her children, she barely earned a hundred rupees a month. Years later, when Subhasini Mistry recounted those early years after she had lost her husband and had had to become provider and protector of her family, she revealed that she had suffered immensely, and had often gone hungry herself so that her children had enough to eat.

'There is no work my hands have not done,' Subhasini recalled. Apart from doing work as a housemaid, she turned her hand to any opportunity she could get to give her children a better life. She worked in a tea stall, cleaned ponds, laboured in paddy fields, collected and carried coal, and sold footwear on the streets, just so that she could earn money for necessities.

When she realised that she would still not make enough to have funds to educate her children, she sent her eldest son Ajoy, even at that tender age a very bright boy, to an orphanage in Bishnupur where he could get a good education. Not having had an education herself, Subhasini was determined that all her children must have a basic education. She recalls begging for schoolbooks and school supplies from people, and although it was a struggle, she was able to send all her four children to school.

Though Subhasini slaved away as a domestic help, she kept her eyes and ears open for fresh opportunities and soon realised that she could earn more money by selling vegetables than as a domestic helper. While Ajoy was at the orphanage, Subhasini moved to Dhapa village along with her three other children and set up a vegetable stall. Business became brisk at her stall and, heartened by this success, Subhasini took another leap of faith and decided to move to the busy city of Kolkata. She set up a small wayside vegetable stall on a bridge in Park Circus in Central

Kolkata and was soon earning more money than she had ever done before.

Subhasini was able to open a savings account in the local post office, depositing small sums of money into it wherever possible. With a small but steady source of income, Subhasini was finally able to focus on the dream that still burnt brightly in her heart. She worked as she had always done, selling vegetables in her humble little wayside stall, and scrimping and saving. She maintained a frugal lifestyle, never spending on anything except the bare necessities. Years later, when asked how she coped with living a tough, hand-to-mouth existence and pursuing her dream, she replied that God had given her the vision and inner strength at the darkest moment of her life, and she remembered those times to motivate herself and keep going.

Each day for twenty years, Subhasini slogged doggedly until she had saved twenty thousand rupees. In 1992, she heard of a one-acre plot of land available for sale in Hanspukur, her late husband's village, and set out to meet the landowner. Subhasini told the landowner of her plans for a hospital for the poor and asked him to sell her the land at a reduced price. The landowner agreed, and sold the land to her for ten thousand rupees. And so, after decades of struggle, Subhasini Mistry had finally taken the first big step towards making her dream come true.

But more challenges lay ahead. Although she had acquired the land for her hospital, Subhasini had little else. Being a seasoned, doughty fighter, Subhasini began to share with the people of Hanspukur her vision for building a village hospital that would provide medical care for those in need regardless of their economic plight.

Subhasini's passion and conviction convinced the villagers, and the first public funds collection began when several families contributed about nine hundred rupees towards the project. Those who had no money contributed their own labour or brought raw material like wood or bamboo and offered their services in construction. A year later, in 1993, with all this goodwill and the savings that remained after the land had been paid for, Subhasini was able to erect a small shed with a mud floor measuring four hundred square feet.

By this time, Ajoy had progressed with his education and, in 1995, qualified as a medical doctor at Kolkata Medical College. Ajoy received huge support from the orphanage, but his path to becoming a doctor was also one of hardship and struggle.

Before being sent away to the orphanage, Subhasini found menial jobs for Ajoy to help bring in a little money to enable the family to survive. At one time in his early teens, the young Ajoy worked as a dishwasher at a tea stall. One day, Ajoy broke a glass while washing and the stall owner punished him by hitting him on his head and face. The heartless man not only ignored Ajoy's piteous tears but also sacked him from the job he so desperately needed. In another job, he was engaged as a domestic help in a large and wealthy family in Hanspukur. One day, he was sent to the market to buy fruit and vegetables. Twelve-year-old Ajoy could not resist the temptation of spending ten paisa to buy a sweet sapota to assuage the pangs of his own hunger. When his employers found out about the missing ten paisa, they were enraged and Ajoy was severely thrashed. Recounting the incident decades later in an interview, Ajoy remembered sadly that, 'No one rescued me even though I was crying profusely. The locals knew the story behind my thrashing, but no one supported me.'

Subhasini found other jobs for young Ajoy, but they were all difficult, many ending in humiliation and even thrashings. Ajoy says that he always looked shabby and unkempt because of poverty and the fact that the family did not have enough for him to even afford decent clothes. Sadly, Ajoy's ragged appearance earned him the cruel and disparaging nickname 'dustbin boy'.

However, things began to look up for Ajoy once he was sent away to the orphanage at Bishnupur. The man who ran the orphanage, Jyotish Chandra Ray, was a kind and generous man. He took Ajoy under his wing and even allowed the bright young boy to live in his home while he studied in school. Ajoy excelled at his studies and passed his school final examination with distinction. He also succeeded on the tough college entrance test and was awarded a German scholarship to study medicine at the Kolkata Medical College. Even while he was a student himself, Ajoy helped other underprivileged boys by tutoring and guiding them with their studies.

Upon graduating from medical school in 1995, Ajoy and a few friends asked some other doctors who they knew to offer free medical services for a few hours every week in Subhasini's new but quite simple hospital. Dr Raghupathy Chatterjee, a cardiologist, was one of the first doctors to respond to this call. Soon after, besides a general physician, specialists in the fields of paediatrics, orthopaedics, ophthalmology, and homeopathy also agreed to help the newly founded clinic, aptly called the Humanity Hospital. And so, on the very first day, in this temporary clinic in a makeshift shed, a total of 252 patients were seen and treated. Subhasini remembers that day vividly. Her eyes welled up with tears on seeing poor patients lining up for treatment at the door. Her dream had truly begun to take shape.

However, this was just the beginning, for Subhasini quickly realised that it would be impossible to run a successful hospital from a ramshackle shed with a thatched roof. The fierce Bengal monsoon meant that water seeped through the roof, damaged precious supplies and equipment, and flooded the premises to the point of being unusable. It was clear that a robust building with solid walls and floor and a sound waterproof roof were a must to run a hospital. To achieve this, more money was needed.

As usual, Subhasini, armed with steely determination, went back stoically to selling vegetables. But this time she was helped by one of her other sons, Sujoy, who too had graduated from college. The mother and son pair worked hard so that they could earn and save more.

Dr Ajoy Mistry, in the meantime, tried to meet the local Member of Parliament (MP), Malini Bhattacharya, to enlist her support. At first she seemed disinterested, not giving Ajoy a hearing. But this did not put the doughty young man off – after all, he was the son of a determined woman. Ajoy persevered and, finally, when the MP saw at first-hand the incredible service being provided to ordinary people from the one-room Humanity Hospital, she was won over. Thus, Malini Bhattacharya became a big supporter of the hospital, and even helped Ajoy raise funds.

Armed with initial success, Ajoy also began to visit corporate houses, would-be well-wishers and charitable organisations to seek support and donations. Just as word continued to spread of the humane work and public service performed by the hospital, more funds began to flow in. Dr Ajoy Mistry, who had watched his mother toil tirelessly all through his childhood, set up 'Humanity Trust' and was able to raise eighty thousand rupees for his mother's dream hospital; and thus, in 1995, the foundation stone for the permanent hospital building was laid. Funds continued to come in at a steady pace and a year later, on 9 March 1996, the two-storeyed Humanity Hospital was inaugurated by the then Governor of West Bengal, K. V. Raghunath Reddy.

Today, the Humanity Hospital covers a floor area of around fifteen hundred square metres and stands on three acres of land. The facilities include all the major branches of medicine such as gynaecology, cardiology, ENT, urology, oncology, diabetology, and surgery, and it also has an intensive care unit. The hospital, still run purely on donations, is managed by a group of trustees that includes medical professionals, local citizens, and serving Indian Police Service (IPS) officers, who provide advice and guidance in the day-to-day running of the hospital. The hospital is accessible to the broadest spectrum of people, with need rather than ability to pay being the driver for the provision of medical care. Each year, thousands of poor people receive free or nearly-free treatment at the Humanity Hospital, while there is provision for various major surgical procedures made available for five thousand rupees or less. The motto of the charitable Humanity Hospital is 'We are with You…', where the ellipsis at the end of the motto indicates Subhasini Mistry's open-hearted desire to simply help all those in need in whatever way possible, without expecting any money in return.

Some years ago, the Humanity Hospital was featured in Aamir Khan's popular TV show 'Satyamev Jayate', which triggered even more publicity and through which the Humanity Trust received donations that helped build a second 25-bed hospital in the Sundarbans. This hospital also boasts modern diagnostic facilities and a fully equipped ICU and is a godsend to villagers in the neighbouring areas, as previously the nearest medical help was in a hospital located one hundred and fifty kilometres away. The Humanity Hospital, Hanspukur, played a key part during the COVID-19 crisis when it was designated a government-approved hospital offering specialist care.

As word spread about the charitable work of the Humanity Hospital, Subhasini Mistry's inspiring story also became well known and, naturally, accolades followed. In 2009, Subhasini Mistry was awarded the Godfrey Phillips Bravery Award in the 'mind-of-steel' category and in 2017 she was one of the winners of the 'Women Transforming India Awards' awarded by NITI Aayog, in partnership with MyGov (Government of India's Citizen Engagement Platform) and the United Nations.

The crowning recognition came in 2018 when Subhasini Mistry was conferred the Padma Shri by the Government of India, which she received from President Ram Nath Kovind at a grand ceremony held at Rashtrapati Bhavan, the President's official residence.

Upon receiving the Padma Shri, Subhasini Mistry told the news daily *Times of India* with characteristic humility, 'I am glad the government has recognised my work. But I would be happier if this award influences others to step up and do their bit for society too. As for me, I had already got my reward when the full-scale hospital was constructed, and the first patient was successfully treated.'[1]

Subhasini has no regrets about the fact that she had no money to spend on herself when she was a young mother. She says, 'What is the use of material things like bangles and saris? We can't take them with us when we die. But the happy faces of the cured poor people have given me such joy and meaning in this life.'

Dr Ajoy Mistry, who got his MD degree in general medicine from Kolkata Medical College in 1997 continues as Chairman of the Humanity Hospital. Though he endured much hardship during childhood, he totally bought into his mother's dream and, along with her, he has striven to live it, work for it, bring it to fruition, and nurture it into becoming what it is today.

'My mother's hard work has always been my strength,' he said in an interview to *The Week* magazine: 'But the hospital was the result of my relentless struggle, through torture and insult. I have felt poverty and humiliation. It prompted me to try and make a difference in society.' When he was asked, in the same interview, how he felt about treating the very same villagers who had years ago thrashed, taunted, and insulted him, Dr Ajoy replied, with rare maturity and understanding, 'Some have apologised, but I tell them that they are not guilty. I was the victim of a society that taught them to do so.'[2]

Three years ago, Dr Ajoy persuaded his mother to stop selling vegetables, as she was getting on in age. Subhasini agreed and began to spend more time in the beloved hospital where she speaks to and reassures patients, giving them succour. One of Subhasini's two daughters and Dr Ajoy Mistry's wife are trained nurses who both work in the hospital. Subhasini says of the Humanity Hospital, 'This hospital means everything to me. It is my wealth, my knowledge, my happiness.'

Subhasini Mistry's remarkable story illustrates 'the Power of One'. Sometimes it takes just one person with the right attitude to change the world and make it a better place. It is a reminder to us that even in times of great trials and hardship, the human spirit has the capacity to rise to seemingly insurmountable challenges. From the tragic loss of her husband rose a vision; a great idea took shape and became the reality of Subhasini's life. With single-minded determination, stoicism and perseverance, Subhasini has achieved something that once looked completely impossible.

'I will not live forever,' Subhasini Mistry says. 'But my hospital will always give free medical treatment to people in need.'

3

Singing the Songs of Life: Sukri Bommagowda

Mythili Rao

It was 2017. Into the grandeur of the Darbar Hall of Rashtrapati Bhavan stepped an elderly woman draped in a saree, with shoulders bare except for a cascade of colourful bead necklaces, her face serenely weather-worn, yet beautiful, adorned with a nose stud and earrings, making her way along the polished marble floor. The generous applause was fitting, for the Darbar Hall, formerly known as the hallowed throne room, the hub of power of empire and the preserve of colonial ceremony, was once again affirming itself as a place of the people and for the people.

The President's guest was Sukri Bommagowda, a remarkable woman who has played such a significant role in keeping one of the countless traditions of India alive. How apposite that the Indian republic's first citizen should invite and honour a fellow citizen into a space whose architect, Edwin Lutyens, barely a century ago, had voiced a contemptuous, colonial opinion of Indians, when he declared the exalted status of his creation and that he had not designed it to 'accommodate all manner of riff-raff and scum'.

Suddenly the spotlight was not just on Sukriji, as she is fondly known, but also on everything that she stood for – the folk tradition that she had for so long nurtured and popularised, the Halakki community that she belonged to, the land around Badageri in Uttara Kannada where they lived, and the significance in the recognition being given to her art and its practice within the Indian cultural landscape.

In the six years since that day at Rashtrapati Bhavan, the spotlight has stayed on Sukriji. Yet, this simple woman whose work in folk music has become the stuff of legend lives in a modest home in the village of Badageri, near Ankola in Uttara Kannada district, Karnataka, where she was born in 1942 into a family of Halakki Vokkaliga, a regional Vanvasi community numbering some 1.5 million. A huge hoarding, with a smiling Sukriji, adorns the wall outside the main street facing her home, as if it had been put there to guide visitors.

Sukriji's family has got used to strangers walking in to meet her and say hello. Fame, it seems, has no barriers. Upon my arrival, I am ushered in without fuss by her daughter-in-law and warmly received by the gentle, innocent smile and twinkling eyes of a folk legend.

Sukriji was sitting on the bed, an oxygen cylinder behind her indicative of declining health since she started suffering from an illness a year ago. The room felt inviting and lived-in despite being a little dusty with a few cobwebs in the upper reaches. The walls were adorned with awards and felicitations indicating the popularity that Sukriji enjoys. During my visit, I discovered that a more spacious room, adjacent to her bedroom-cum-visitors-room, is decorated with more awards, photographs of her with popular personalities, cuttings of newspaper articles and other paraphernalia of Sukriji's amazing life journey.

In conversation, Sukriji is simple and direct, warm and caring. She mentioned that, well before she became famous, professors and students of folk culture from Hampi University would invite her to perform and talk about her folk songs. The Padma Shri changed all that and brought not just herself but her community into the national limelight. 'I was singing for decades before Padma Shri and have continued singing after Padma Shri. I have not changed in my art as a result of the recognition. The award came to me because I was singing. It has not influenced me in any way except that now people recognise me and keep coming to meet me.'

Like many of her Halakki kinsfolk, Sukriji's family was immersed in the folk music that has been passed down across several generations. I learn that she was named Sukri on account of being born on a Friday – *Shukravaaraa*. Father Subba played the *gumate*, a traditional clay-pot-shaped percussion instrument with a leather skin and he was well known as a performer of the Suggi folk dance. Her mother, Devi, was famed locally for the innumerable folk songs she sang while working in the fields, often accompanied by Sukriji's elder sister. With such a musically filled atmosphere at home, it was inevitable that the young Sukri would be drawn towards the art from early in life.

The absence of a formal education was no barrier to learning, and in the true spirit of sustaining and growing through tradition, she grew up playing folk games like *atta-atta*, *pagade*, and *kattaata* and also learnt the songs of her Halakki forebears, passed down orally in Halakki Kannada or Achchagannada, a dialect of Kannada, from her mother. As with children in many communities, Sukri helped with tasks which have for eons been part of rural life, collecting cow-dung and firewood, and joining the family working both in the home and the fields. Being close to nature gave the young Sukri plenty of opportunity to explore her world. Field and forest became familiar friends. She learnt not only the names of the various plants and trees but also about their medicinal properties whose secrets had been passed down among the Halakki since the dawn of time.

Life has not been easy for Sukriji. As per the Halakki tradition, her parents arranged for Sukri to be married at the tender age of fourteen. Sadly, her then forty-five-year-old agricultural labourer husband was an alcoholic and both he and the two sons she bore died while she herself was still young. Even a boy that she had adopted died later due to alcoholic poisoning. These tragic events had a great impact on Sukri, as evidenced by the causes that she took up later in life.

Folk literature everywhere is made up of song and story handed down the generations through oral tradition. Sukri began learning the Halakki folk songs from her mother and elder sister and, in our conversation, she remembered that the first song she memorised was the song sung for Govinda, the devata or god the Halakki revere.

Shorn of the trappings of the urban, mechanised setting or the sense of importance that one finds in some present-day artists, Sukriji spontaneously broke into the song she had first learnt from her mother. In the quiet environs of her home, with the cackling of the hens, mooing of the cows tethered in a shed somewhere in the vicinity, and the banter of womenfolk, the dry rustic voice carried the rich heritage of an ancient people. Unaccompanied by any instrument or embellishment, she transforms into the lovely, feminine Tulsi getting herself ready to meet her divine elder brother Govinda.

ಬಣ್ಣ ಉಡುವುದು, ಮಂಡೆ ಕಟ್ಟೋದು, ಚಿನ್ನ ಹಾಕೋದು,, ಅಪ್ಪನ ಮನೆಗೆ
ಹೋಗೋದು
ಹೂವಿನ ಮೂಡುವಲ್ಲೆಗಮನವೇ ಕೊಡುವೆ ಚಿನ್ನವ ಇಡುವಲ್ಲೆಗಮನವೇ
ಚಿನ್ನ ಇಡುವಲ್ಲೆಗಮನವೇ ತೋಲು ಚಮಣೆ ಗಂಡಲೇ ಇದು ಗಮನವೇ
ಗಂಡವ್ಯೆಡುವಲ್ಲೆಗಮನವೇ ತೋಲು ಚಮ್ಮನೆ ಅಪ್ಪನ ಮನೆಗ್ ಹೋಗು ಗಮನವೇ
ಅಪ್ಪನಮನೆ ಹೋಗ ಗಮನವೇ ತೋಳು ಚಮ್ಮನೇ ಕೈಯಲ್ಲಜೋಡಿ ತಲೆದಲೋ

Wearing colourful clothes, tying up the hair with flowers,
Adorned in gold, I am going to Father's home....

The song continues reverberating through Sukriji's rustic voice until it becomes clear to the listener that *Chammane* is Lord Govinda, Lord Tirupati, Shri Krishna Himself, who is venerated as an elder brother, for in this song, which is usually sung during *Tulsi Puja*, Govinda is addressed as '*Anna*', elder brother in Kannada. The lyrics poetically describe the adornments of Govinda, his gracious features and divine character, the devotion that everyone has for him, and the rituals followed in the puja. The song's melody is simple, the repetition of some words adding to its rhythm and pace, while the main lyrics express cultural emotions that are at the same time popular and rooted in identity. In fact, the song was such a pleasant surprise for me that, as Sukriji continued singing, I felt as if I had transformed into Tulsi and was undergoing all the motions presented in the song.

On finishing the last couplet of the song, Sukriji continues, 'There cannot be any occasion without a song, whether life or death, festival or mourning, welcoming the spring or rain, even fetching water or farming has a song. Why, if a song does not already exist for the occasion, then one must create one!'

Not content with the many songs that she had learnt from her mother, Sukriji has created hundreds of her own songs.

She recalled that, even as a youngster, she loved creating songs. The melodies of nature, whether when helping in the fields or playing folk games, or simply listening to the sounds of the forest, all became stimuli for her musical education.

Over the years, beyond the spiritual lyrics connecting to the divine, Sukriji's simple yet powerful lyric compositions have also addressed important social matters like education, alcoholism and so on. Adorned with *mani* beads necklaces, a symbol of Halakki culture, with saree tied tightly in the Halakki *okkalagate* style, rhythmically beating the leather-capped *gumate* while singing and dancing, Sukriji has become the true representative of her rich tradition and is known throughout India as 'Nightingale of Halakki'.

Television documentaries made around Sukriji's life and work have gained her much popularity across Karnataka, and in the process, she has acquired the accolade of 'Halakki cuckoo'. She has worked with the Karnataka Folk Academy that has compiled a book of her songs. Karwar Radio has recorded many of her songs so that they may be preserved and promoted to carry forward the tradition, while her life story is now part of the Karnataka school curriculum.

Sukriji's contributions and successes are not limited to her musical legacy, however. Her experiences have shaped her life beyond the artistic with forays into activities leading to the betterment of not just her small community but also society at large.

While being recognised as a 'face' of the Halakki community, Sukriji was motivated to contest local elections and on winning she became a member of the Badageri Gram Panchayat or Village Council. In this role, she was empowered to work on various initiatives for the change and betterment of her community.

Many of the Halakki live in traditional homes called *hullu mane*, a simple house made of thatch and mud.

On becoming a Panchayat member, Sukriji took personal responsibility for getting forty-five concrete homes constructed for her kinsfolk in Badageri.

Having had to endure the tragedy of the drink-induced deaths of the men in her life, Sukriji knew first hand the evil that alcoholism causes among rural and Vanvasi communities. She therefore made it a mission to curtail alcohol abuse and campaigned for better education and information within the community, galvanising Halakki women to fight against alcoholism and pressure local government to close liquor shops in the area.

Another cause that is close to Sukriji's heart is education. Having missed out on the opportunity to go to school in her childhood, Sukriji has used her own life as an example to motivate families within her community to educate their children, believing that preserving traditions and yet being schooled are entirely compatible and necessary for the times. Sukriji's regret is that, after formal education with its evident material benefits, some of the younger generation within the Halakki community become less interested in learning and preserving their culture that is so colourfully exhibited in songs, dance and games.

'They are learning English now, they don't want to work in the fields, wear the bead strings or the saree like us,' Sukriji laments. 'Perhaps, it is all over now!' she says, in a matter of fact, sad manner, echoing the sentiments of many who belong to the generation of this delightful eighty-two-year-old.

Though some senior members of the community and teachers in the local schools are striving hard to teach children these arts, it remains an uphill task. To complement local initiatives, Sukriji also visits schools in Bengaluru, Mysore, Hampi, Mangaluru, and many of the smaller towns of Karnataka to spread awareness and pass on knowledge of Halakki songs and traditions. However, Sukriji remains pessimistic, fearing that modernity and 'progress' will mean that her legacy may die.

India, with its rich tapestry of diversity has many small communities whose unique traditions and lifestyles are increasingly under pressure from the double-edged sword of material progress and modernity. The Halakki are no exception, and so Sukriji is actively campaigning for the community to be recognised as a scheduled tribe so that they can benefit from the protections and support from special schemes provided in Indian law. To back this up, Sukriji placed a formal request on behalf of the Halakki community before Prime Minister Shri Narendra Modi during his visit to her village in 2023.

Sukriji has also requested the Prime Minister for a well-equipped local hospital to meet the needs of the people of Ankola who currently need to travel significant distances for medical care. She is quietly confident that the hospital will soon be a reality. Demonstrating confidence and faith in the Prime Minister, she said, 'He is a very capable man with heart.'

On a more general level, Sukriji has supported various cross-community cooperation initiatives, among which is the Kote Bavi movement. In 2017, she walked in solidarity with the movement across North Karnataka from Ankola to Karwar in a campaign to have the Halakki included among the Scheduled Tribes category to access government-supported community development opportunities. The movement drew positive public attention and, in some circles, the initiative was equated with the famous Dandi march in pre-Independent India.

During our conversation, Sukriji's thoughts turn to mother and nature.

She talks passionately, expressing her utmost regard for Mother, and sees her form in Nature too. She says,

'A mother is like God because she nurtures the unborn child in her womb for nine months, and then once the child comes to this world, she still nourishes the child, bathing, feeding, singing to it, keeping it close to her heart, protecting it by applying a black spot to ward off the evil eye, cradling it on her lap, raising it to be an independent adult.'

Talking of her own childhood, she reminisces fondly about her mother. 'Her giving me life and bringing me up is one debt that I can never repay. In fact, no one can repay the debt they owe their Mother.' When asked what she remembers about her mother today, she smiles and says with joy that her mother would have been very happy today. 'There is no God greater than the Mother.' But then she becomes somewhat sombre, continuing, 'Today everything seems to have changed. Nobody wants father or mother. People are only interested in themselves, a wife, and their children.'

According to Sukriji, 'Woman and Nature are the sustaining forces of life itself.'

As per Halakki tradition, Sukriji is firm in her faith in Govinda, Lord Tirupati and Tulsi and, just as in every household among her kinsfolk, her home too has a '*kari devaru*', a black stone symbolising the Supreme Deity and a Tulsi plant.

She recalls many of the individuals who have, over the decades, been helpful to her not just in cash and kind but in believing in her, offering her avenues in which to grow, to be creative, and, above all, to live a life full of possibilities. Sukriji's travels have made her worldly-wise, yet still connected with her kinsfolk, understanding their needs and aspirations. She is contented with her life.

The daughter-in-law comes to remind Sukriji of some guests with schoolchildren who are expected shortly. To prepare her for it, she had brought the cascading yellow bead necklace beads, which she places around the elder's neck. While she does this, and as if speaking to herself, she mildly complains that the string has become too tight. 'A lady who had come from Karwar had borrowed this for some programme, and when she returned it, it has somehow become tight for Ajji. It is clear that the threading that binds the multiple strings had been replaced.'

Sukriji ended our meeting with some profound thoughts: 'Every human is God. We are one. In this, *jaati*, tribe, and clan do not matter. We do not have a say. It is His wish as to how long I live. We fold our hands in veneration and offer puja to all the deities but our tradition rests with faith in Tulsi. We enter the world in darkness and go naked. In our interactions with others, we need to show gentleness, speak in a manner that avoids hurt, promotes respect.'

'What wise words!' I think to myself as I sit in front of this unassuming, simple, yet amazing woman, gasping in awed silence.

Here is a someone whose thoughts echo the humane philosophy of many Rishis and Saints whose footprints have graced this land – wisdom of thought and living in practice that even the best formal education cannot easily buy. A true Padma Shri of Bharat.

We bid each other goodbye with folded hands.

Sukriji may be in poor health, yet her zest for life remains shining. I pray that she will live forever.

Sukriji has been recognised by various government and private bodies for her contribution to the enrichment of folk traditions. By the time she had the Padma Shri conferred on her in 2017, she had already been honoured with the Janapada Shri Award by Government of Karnataka (1999), the Nadoja Award by Kannada University, Hampi (2006), the Sandesh Kala Award (2009), and the Alwas Nudisiri Award by Karnataka Folk Academy (2009). She is also the recipient of the 'Van Suma' Award in the presence of Sri Sri Sowmyanatha Swamiji of Sri Adichunchanagiri Bengaluru Math in July 2017.

4

Rekindling Kalaripayattu: A Spotlight on India's Forgotten Heritage

Patañjali Pundit

For six decades following the nation's declaration of Independence, Kalaripayattu lay neglected – a forgotten treasure buried in the sands of time, its brilliance shrouded in obscurity.

'What is Kalaripayattu?' you may ask. It is an ancient Indian martial art that originated and flourished in Kerala. At its zenith, the practitioners of the art form achieved extraordinary feats of combat and physical prowess, and its influence extended far beyond the training grounds, leaving an indelible mark on India's cultural heritage.

Legend has it that Kalaripayattu can trace its lineage to Sage Parashuram, subject of popular tales deeply etched into the cultural memory of the Indian subcontinent. In one such story, the revered hermit stood atop a mountain in Konkan and with his divine axe cleaved through the waters of the Arabian Sea. He reclaimed from the ocean a verdant paradise on India's southwestern coast, known today as Kerala. The story continues further and credits him for consecrating forty-two centres across Kerala for teaching the art of Kalaripayattu to disciples from different Brahman families. Codified in the 11th century, Kalaripayattu at its peak radiated with unparalleled glory, seamlessly weaving a tapestry of physical mastery, spiritual wisdom and cultural eminence. With the arrival of foreign powers, the flourishing training centres gradually faded into memory.

Fast-forward to present times and, thanks to the visionary endeavours of the Central government, Kalaripayattu is experiencing a renaissance. In 2017, Meenakshi Amma, a living legend of Kalari, received the prestigious Padma Shri award. This accolade marked the very first time that a martial art form had been recognised in such a manner. Two other luminaries, Shri Sankarnarayanan Menon and Shri S.R.D. Prasad, in 2022 and 2023 respectively, received the Padma Shri award in recognition of their unwavering commitment to this venerable discipline. The Indian government, recognising its invaluable practicality in modern combat scenarios, has made Kalaripayattu an integral part of training programmes for its specialised armed forces.

I embarked upon a profound journey to the homeland of Kalaripayattu in pursuit of unveiling the enigmatic essence of this ancient martial art. The remarkable life stories of the three distinguished individuals bestowed with the Padma Shri award would serve as beacons guiding me through this illuminating pilgrimage.

Keeping in tune with the Indic traditions, I decided to visit the luminaries in the chronological order of their age, eldest first and youngest last.

Custodians of Tradition

The first stop on my quest to uncover the history of Kalaripayattu was Chavakkad, the small town adjoining the popular Guruvayur Temple. What better place to start my pilgrimage than a temple town. Chavakkad is also home to Vallabhatta Kalari Sangham, led by Shri Sankarnarayana Menon, a 2022 Padma Shri awardee. His father, the late Virasree Sankunni Panikkar Gurukkal, had established Vallabhatta after moving to Chavakkad. Sankuni Gurukkal was helped by his four sons, Ravunnikutty, Sreedhara, Sankaranarayana, and Viswanathan. At the behest of one Shri Meleppura R. Vishwanathan, a friend of the Pannikar kutumb (family), Vishwanathan was enlisted as a sparring partner to provide Kalari instruction. Meleppura R.V. later assisted the Pannikar family in setting up Vallabhatta Kalari Sangham. It was sheer fortune that I found myself under the hospitality of the amiable Gautham Meleppura, the grandson of Meleppura R.V. However, upon my arrival, Gautham shared sombre tidings that the nonagenarian master of Kalari had passed away just two months previously. It was a setback, but I made my way to Vallabhatta to learn as much as I could about Sankarnarayan Menon.

Unni Gurukkal, as Menon was popularly known, was ninety-three and already a local celebrity when he received the award. His students, from all walks of life, can be found in not just Kerala but across Europe. Trained by his father, Unni Gurukkal had dedicated his life to promoting the traditional practice of Kalaripayattu. He is survived by a wife, a daughter and three sons, all Kalaripayattu experts. Krishnadas, being the eldest, manages Vallabhatta with his brothers, Rajiv and Dinesh. He still carries the sorrow of his father's passing but was delighted at the opportunity to talk about Unni Gurukkal's legacy and Vallabhatta.

A Sacred Space

Walking into the Vallabhatta Kalari with Krishnadas felt like walking into a sanctum sanctorum. 'It is a temple of learning, a sacred space,' he points out matter-of-factly as he heads straight to the southwest corner that houses the *Poothra*, seven crimson-coloured steps. 'The seven steps are the seven mother deities,' he explains. Pointing from the bottom-most step, he continues, 'Brahmi, Vaishnavi, Maheswari, Varahi, Indrani, Kaumari, Chamundi. At the top is Shiva-Shakti.' Every Kalari has a *Poothra*, a *thala* (place) for Vighneshwara and guru. These three are the minimum requisite *thalas*. A Kalari is about seven metres wide, fourteen metres long and seven metres high. In accordance with Vaastu principles, the main door is in the east and an additional door in the north.

A Kalari is where you learn *sadhana*, training the body with exercises repeatedly until one attains perfection. These days, individuals approach Kalaris like Vallabhatta with requests for a three- to six-month crash course. However, Krishnadas says that an emphatic stance is maintained to resist such requests. During the initial few months, the focus is exclusively on body control exercises, a crucial foundation in the practice. 'Only the guru can decide when you are ready to progress to the next step. This is called *Chuvadamattam*,' Krishnadas adds. He then explains to me in detail the four stages of Kalaripayattu. Upon mastering the four stages, the Gurukkal tests the *shishya*'s discipline, mind–body *Ekagratha* (oneness) and faith in the Gurukkal. This is done to deem whether the *shishya* is worthy enough to be initiated into *Marma–Chikitsa* and *Uzhichil* (knowledge of the vital points). This final stage goes beyond massage and treatment as commonly perceived. Hitting the vital points with his bare hands a Kalari master could disarm or even kill an enemy.

'It Runs in Our Blood'
Quoting in chaste Malayalam from the family's palm-leaf text, Krishnadas tells me about his family's history. Unni

Gurukkal was the third son of the late Gurukkal Sankunni Panicker, the last member of the Mudavangatil family, who was made the *anchaimakaimal* (commander-in-chief) by the Vettath Raja with responsibility for both training those who would fight on the Raja's behalf and for eradication of malevolence in their region.

'I am the eighth generation and my daughters the ninth. Kalaripayattu is our life, it runs in our blood,' Krishnadas proudly proclaims.

Unni Gurukkal was initiated into Kalari at the age of four, started demonstrations at sixteen, and had trained almost a hundred thousand (lakh) students over the course of his lifetime. 'From the moment Papa woke up in the morning to the moment before going to bed, he was always talking about Kalari, quoting *sholkas* or describing movements,' I am told. He was a simple man who had dedicated his life to the promotion of Kalaripayattu. His students remember him to have been a 'very strict guru but a very kind man'. His teachings were not limited to exercises; he would explain to students the philosophy involved too. For most of his former students he was more than just a martial art teacher. Such was the love and respect his students had for Menon that a number of them accompanied him to Delhi for the Padma Shri.

'Papa had been awarded many awards over his lifetime but once I came across a notification for sending nominations for Padma Shri, I got to work,' Krishnadas declares. Lacking recommendations from any politician or bureaucrat, it took him more than three months of data and document collection to nominate his father. 'My joy knew no bounds when I read "Shri Sankarnarayan Menon, Chundayil" scrolling with his picture on the television as they announced the awardees. It was a fitting culmination of his life's work,' a teary-eyed Krishnadas conveys to me in a heavy voice standing in the middle of the Kalari. 'Vallabhatta is no longer just the name of a school. It has evolved into a brand that symbolises tradition in the 21st century, all due to his hard work,' he confidently asserts. 'My only wish is that he could have lived to a 100.'

The Knowledge-Keeper

In a small corner in a residential locale, in the seaside town of Kannur, is an unassuming building called the Sree Bharat Kalari. In a plain square room with a table, a chair, a bench, and a bookcase next to the Kalari building sits the affable S.R.D. Prasad Gurukkal, the 2023 recipient of Padma Shri for Kalaripayattu. Son of the legendary Chirakkal T. Sreedharan Nair, Prasad Gurukkal is an inexhaustible resource for all things Kalari. He begins by narrating the legend of Parashuram and the creation of Kerala. 'Even if historians discard this as myth born of a fanciful imagination, historic facts can be read as legend,' says Prasad Gurukkal. 'Bharagava Rama is said to be the Parashuram of legend. So, this is history. The forest land was cleared with axes and agriculture began in Kerala.'

A Syncretic Origin Story

As Prasad continues, he delves into the historical origins of Kalaripayattu in the Sangam-era[1] when the Chera, Chola and Pandyas fought for dominance over the Deccan peninsula, and takes me on a journey through history right up to Kalaripayattu's relevance today.

A striking feature of south India was the prevalence of hero-worship. Martial champions were deified if fallen in battle, their ballads sung and *virakkals* (memorials) erected in their honour. 'Sangam literature speaks of warriors trained with *vel* (spear), *val* (sword) and *kedaham* (shield), and *vil* (bow) – weapons still used in Kalaripayattu,' he points out. Over time, the syncretism of the pan-Indian martial tradition of Dhanur-veda that accompanied migrations from Konkan merged with local traditions and evolved into a codified structure known as Kalaripayattu.

Historians have established that, by the 7th century CE, the Malabar region was dotted with institutions known as *Salai*,[2] the precursors of the Kalaris that exist today. The *Salai* played a critical function in the development of a distinctive linguistic and cultural identity for Kerala. The term Kalaripayattu itself and its associated *Vayattharis* (oral commands for exercises) emerged in tandem with the crystallisation of a distinct Malayalam language.[3] Over time, with the establishment of social functions within and amongst communities, the Brahmans limited themselves to the study of *shastras*. The art of Kalaripayattu was passed to other communities who gained expertise in it and paved the way for the golden era of Kalaripayattu.

Of Ballads and Duels

Our chief resource for knowledge of Kalaripayattu in this era[4] is the *Vadakkan Pattukal*, folk ballads that glorify Kalari warriors.[5] The *Vadakkan Pattukal* also mention heroines of Kalari and experts from all segments of Hindu society, as well as Muslims, suggesting that gender, *jaati* and common biases were non-existent in Kalari.

Kerala seems to have been largely untouched by the great wars that took place between kingdoms in most parts of India due to a decentralised system of governance that mostly led to small skirmishes between principalities. The paramount position of Kalari can be gauged from the fact that a well-defined system of warfare had developed called *ankam* (duel to death). But Kalari was not limited to warfare between kingdoms and chieftains. An *ankam* centric system of conflict resolution had been put in place. For conflicts between two households, it was called *kutipakka,* and if the dispute was personal, *poithu.*

'When there were feuds, they were taken to *desa-vali* for settlement,' says Prasad Gurukkal. If the *desa-vali* was unresolved, it was taken to the *nadu-vali.* 'But if the matter could not be settled by the *nadu-vali* also, then it was given for *ankam.* Two representatives were chosen for the aggrieved parties who took part in the duel. Was it a just system of dispute resolution? Maybe not,' he continues, 'but quarrels that could result in mass murders between warring/ disagreeing factions could be avoided in this system.'

Death and Rebirth
With the arrival of European powers on the Malabar shores in the 15th century, new weapons and tactics were introduced to the region that posed a threat to the existing traditions. The story of Thatchi Othenan, a legendary hero from the folk ballads and *Theyyams,* serves as a parable.[6] Othenan was a distinguished master of Kalaripayattu, respected even by the Zamorin of Kozhikode. Hot on the heels of his greatest victory in an *ankam* with Kathirur Gurukkal, 32-year-old Othenan was shot dead by one of Kathirur Gurukkal's students. The bullet that killed Othenan represents an apt marker in the inexorable battle leading to the decline of Kalaripayattu and the culture of Kerala.

The next blow to Kalaripayattu came 200 years later, in the late 1750s, with the Islamic conquest of Malabar by Hyder Ali. The invasion brought with it persecutions and forced conversions, disrupting not just Kalaripayattu but the way of life itself, as temples and adjacent Kalaris were razed to the ground. The coup-de-grace for an already weakened tradition happened with the Cotiote War fought between the East India Company and Pazhassi Raja of Kottayam.[7] Exasperated by defeats at the hands of the Kalari-trained Kottayam army with less than half of their strength, the British banned Kalaripayattu in 1804. The very next year, Pazhassi Raja fell. With the introduction of an English education system under British rule, indigenous traditions slowly suffocated.

The revival of Kalaripayattu, according to Prasad, took place during the Swadeshi movement of the Indian freedom struggle. K. Kellappan, popularly known as 'Kerala Gandhi' and a Kalari expert in his own right, spearheaded the revival movement, sowing the seeds for Kalaripayattu's rebirth. From Vadakara in Kozhikode, his rallying cry was to study and practise all indigenous art forms, with Kalaripayattu taking centre stage in his endeavour. 'It was then that my father also introduced himself to Kalaripayattu along with others like C.V.N. Nair. They started their own Kalaris and had their own students,' states Prasad.

S.R.D. Prasad is the son of T. Sreedharan Nair who established his Kalari in 1935. 'It was named Rajkumar Kalari as he considered himself a *Rajkumar* (prince), a homage to his lineage,' says Prasad Gurukkal and laughs. 'In 1948, he renamed it Sree Bharath Kalari and it remains the same to this day.' Sreedharan Nair was initially swayed by the Western physical culture of body-building and muscle control. It was only when one of his friends introduced him to Kalaripayattu that he became interested in traditional martial traditions. He invited various gurus from Vadakkara to Payannur to his house and dedicated himself to learning the martial art. 'He would practise continuously, not one or two hours but morning till evening, and so he managed to learn in a very short span of time.'

The Apple Doesn't Fall Far

Prasad Gurukkal was initiated into Kalari, along with his elder brother, when he was just four years old. They trained under the tutelage of their father, giving multiple demonstrations of Kalari during their time in high school and college. Even while working for the rubber board, Prasad and his troupe were asked to perform for an international audience by an IAS (Indian Administrative Service) officer. Upon retirement, Prasad assumed the mantle of leadership at Sree Bharath Kalari, a position previously held by his father's disciple, Vijay Master. Inspired by the legacy of his father, who had written the very first book on Kalaripayattu in Malayalam in 1935, Prasad has since penned multiple volumes in recent years, including an encyclopaedia dedicated to this ancient martial art.

As a seasoned Kalari expert, in collaboration with Kannur University, Prasad undertook the monumental task of crafting the very first curriculum for Kalari instruction within higher education institutions. Regrettably, this ambitious initiative did not yield the results he had hoped for, and the subject was discontinued after just one year. Nevertheless, Prasad Gurukkal remains resolute in his belief that the preservation of Kalari's rich traditions necessitates their documentation. It is for this dedication to preserve the limitless knowledge of Kalaripayattu that he was awarded the Padma Shri, having been unaware that he had been nominated.

A Legacy of Inclusivity

Undoubtedly, among the three awardees, Meenakshi Raghavan stands out as the most renowned. It took nearly two weeks of persistent effort before I secured an opportunity to visit her, given her popularity and a hectic schedule of demonstrations. Posters with her pictures guided me across Vadakara to Kadathanad Kalari Sangham.

Meenakshi Amma, as she is fondly called, rose to prominence and brought much-needed attention to Kalaripayattu when she received the Padma Shri award in 2017, marking a historic first for this martial art form. A remarkable practitioner of Kalaripayattu, she embarked on her journey into the world of martial arts at the tender age of seven, kindling a lifelong passion for the discipline. Now, aged 80, her commitment to the art form remains unwavering, as she emphatically states in Malayalam – 'until the day I die' – with her granddaughter-in-law, Mahima, kindly translating the sentiment into English for my understanding. Meenakshi Amma is driven by her love for Kalari and her desire to continue her late husband's legacy.

Meenakshi Amma's love for Kalaripayattu was nurtured close to her home, where she started training in 1949. In Meenakshi Amma's own words, 'I started dance at the age of six and began Kalari training at seven.' It was her dance teachers who had advised her father to train her in Kalaripayattu, given her near perfect forms and flexibility at such a tender age. She studied under the able guidance of V.P. Raghavan, who initially served as her guru and nine years later became her life partner. With unwavering determination and guidance from her husband, she achieved a level of excellence honed over decades.

Against All Odds

Kadathanad Kalari Sangham has thrived against all odds and grown into a beacon of tradition and inclusivity. 'When we began, we faced a lot of discrimination as my husband was from the Theeya community. Traditionally, there were different Kalaris for different *jaatis*, but in our Kalari all the communities were welcomed and everybody was accommodated,' she reminisces. Under the faint glow of lanterns held by a handful of dedicated supporters, driven by a potent mixture of anguish and resolute determination, a teenage V.P. Raghavan had dug out the Kadathanad Kalari in a single night. This event had occurred as a direct response to him being denied access to advanced Kalari training on account of him belonging to the Theeya community.

In the early days of Kadathanad, she recalls, 'The Kalari featured a traditional thatched roof of coconut leaves.' However, over the past seven decades and more, it has seen a significant transformation. At one point it featured a modern sheet roof, but today what we see is a solid structure of brick, wood, and concrete, creating a blend of heritage and contemporary design. Initially, there were barely any students and one could count the number of female students on fingertips, but today over 200 students enrol annually, not only martial arts enthusiasts but also doctors, engineers, and housewives, all seeking to master the art of Kalaripayattu. The pride in Meenakshi Amma's voice is evident as she recounts.

Defying Gravity

As a married couple, Meenakshi Amma helped Raghavan master all aspects of running the Kadathanad Kalari. Recalling her journey, she notes, 'After my husband's passing, I took up the mantle, resurrecting the institution with the support of former and new students. My ambition is to maintain my husband's legacy.'

'Over the years, international journalists from leading news outlets, mostly from the US and UK, extensively filmed me, a female martial art practitioner from Kerala,' Meenakshi Amma recalls. These videos captured significant attention owing to her exceptional mastery of the discipline. It was a form of newfound recognition that culminated in her receiving a prestigious award, she believes, as no one had nominated her for it. Her profound joy upon being honoured by the President in the presence of the Prime Minister and other dignitaries was evident. In the depths of her recollections, the memory of that moment remains vivid, perpetually etched as a wellspring of inspiration. 'It fills me with *urjaa* (energy) every time I think about it,' she says, raising her arms in a front double bicep pose sporting a wide grin.

Despite receiving numerous offers to work in cinema, even before Raghavan Master's passing, Meenakshi Amma has remained steadfast in her commitment to Kalaripayattu. She recalls, 'I declined because they would disrupt my work at the Kalari but Rajan Sir requested so persistently that I gave in.' Little did she know that she would have to travel away from Kadathanad for days on end to shoot. 'Won't be doing that again,' she adds, voicing her frustration with the process.[8]

Setting the Bar High

Taking me on a tour of her Kalari, she continues, 'In Kerala, the forms of Kalari are classified according to the local dynasties that existed. Kadathanad Kalari is more a northern style and we adopted Parashuram as the original guru, so at Kadathnad Kalari we teach the *Vadakkan* style with influences from South Kerala.' Amma takes pride in having encouraged numerous women to embrace Kalari, thereby broadening its appeal. Operating with seamless efficiency from morning to night, they maintain a schedule that accommodates three distinct training sessions daily and are determined to sustain this routine.

Remarkably, over the course of seven decades, they have steadfastly upheld a policy of not levying any fees on students and refrained from seeking any financial assistance from government bodies or private organisations, only charging a nominal fee for *Marma–Chikitsa* treatments. However, with an influx of foreign participants, the dynamics have shifted; they have been offered donations to support their cause. The unremunerated tutelage at Kadathanad is intended for the well-being and education of their students, especially those from poor backgrounds, with a primary focus on nurturing both the students and the prolonged perpetuation of Kalari itself.

As the grand matriarch of Kalari ages gracefully, she has ensured that her legacy lives on through an academy in Trivandrum or Thiruvananthapuram, where her former students carry forward the Kadathanad tradition. Meenakshi Amma is vigilant about maintaining the integrity of Kalaripayattu. She voices her concern about individuals claiming to be gurus without genuine expertise, emphasising the importance of proper training to prevent accidents. 'People are learning rudimentary basics for a short time and going outside to teach without full knowledge. Fake Gurukkals!' she says emphatically, shaking her head. She remains committed to providing high standards of education for aspiring Kalaripayattu practitioners, irrespective of how long she can personally continue to teach.

Emergence from the Embers
Much like all *Bharatiya paramparas*, the genesis of Kalaripayattu weaves together threads of myth and history. This ancient martial art is intricately intertwined with the cultural, political and social evolution of Kerala and, to a broader extent, that of Indian history. Even in the face of

British attempts to suppress it, Kalaripayattu demonstrated remarkable resilience, flourishing clandestinely under the skilled stewardship of Gurukkals. In the present day, Kalaripayattu is experiencing a renewed surge in popularity, whilst at the same time having to confront the challenge of accommodating the increasingly hectic schedules of modern students, some of whom aspire to master all four stages of this ancient art form within a single year. The discipline has also undergone evolution to align with year-round training regimens, departing from its traditional seasonal practices.[9]

Emerging from the shadows of history, Kalaripayattu has begun to captivate the hearts and minds of a new generation. Cinematic endeavours that celebrate its legacy serve as an invitation to delve deeper into the world of Kalari. It is as if the art itself has been reborn, capturing the hearts and imaginations of people everywhere, ensuring that this ancient treasure remains an eternal source of fascination and inspiration.

In a conversation with Anmol Mothi, a former disciple of Unni Gurukkal and a local politician, I asked him how Kalaripayattu had transformed his life. His response was swift and resounding: 'Patience. Kalaripayattu doesn't merely impart combat skills,' he explained with an air of grace, a natural consequence of Kalari practice. 'Its core principle revolves around defence but, more importantly, it instils the wisdom of knowing when not to engage in conflict.' This time-honoured discipline with mythic origins initially evolved as a method for combat and dispute resolution. It has, over time, grown into a comprehensive practice that prioritises physical and mental well-being. It is only because of consistent efforts of modern day Gurukkals like Meenakshi Amman, Sankarnarayan Menon, and S.R.D. Prasad that Kalaripayattu's popularity is experiencing a phoenix-like resurgence, a testament to India's indomitable spirit.

5

Ramesh and Shanti Parmar: *Gudiya Karigar* and *Samaj Kalakar ki Jodi*

Munmun Banerjee

A serene twilight welcomes Ramesh and Shanti Parmar, recently honoured with the prestigious Padma Shri, as chief guests at the handicraft exhibition in Ujjain with the ancient *shikara* of the Jyoytirling Mahakaleshwar Mandir offering a divine backdrop for the occasion.

The Parmar couple, recognised for their profound contributions to keeping alive and promoting traditional handicrafts, address a large gathering. Among the locals and visitors to this famous city of Shiva, there are dignitaries and administrators, artisans and eager reporters.

As the gentle hum of the present moment fades, I feel myself being pulled into their story, which I have only recently read about. The full reality of Ramesh and Shanti's captivating tale unfolds that evening, drawing me deeper into their world, one that has planted its roots in the quaint town of Jhabua, Madhya Pradesh, close to the trisection with neighbouring Gujarat and Maharashtra.

The intricate tapestry of Jhabua revolves around the Bhil community, who make up the largest group in the town and surrounding areas. Eternally famed for Sabri, the simple devotee of Maryada Purshottam Ram in the Ramayana, the Bhil are spread across central India. Under 19th-century British colonialist-implemented social engineering and racial determinism laws, scores of India's diverse communities numbering in the millions came to be classified, categorised and demarcated by the colonial rulers as 'dangerous classes' and 'criminal castes'. Deemed to be a law-and-order problem, they were formally criminalised under the Criminal Tribes Act (CTA) and faced arrest and imprisonment without cause, with restrictions on where they could live or work. Children were sometimes forcibly separated from families for 'reformatory' purposes.

This legacy lingers, and the Bhil still face prejudice, which is further intensified by Jhabua's unfortunate levels of crime. Poverty and unemployment, and especially the recent licensing of locally produced Mahua liquor, have amplified societal complexities, inadvertently driving liquor smuggling and providing an easy escape for criminals across state borders.

And, yet, amidst this backdrop, Ramesh and Shanti Parmar have for decades, stood out as transformative figures, challenging norms and working at the grassroots to bring about positive change.

The bus halts at Jhabua where the Parmars have been eagerly waiting to meet me. Ramesh, donned in a simple kurta pajama, welcomes me with a genuine smile while Shanti, elegantly attired in a colourful saree with her head covered in a flowing *pallu*, offers a respectful namaste, her nimble hands bearing marks of countless artistic pursuits.

We navigate through the labyrinth of narrow lanes, and arrive in a street with a close, tightly packed cluster of houses decorated in various colours. One house, distinct yet harmoniously nestled among the cluster, catches my eye.

Its walls were rough and weatherworn, bearing witness to the passage of many monsoons. Set within the rustic texture of the front wall is a gleaming new addition: a rectangular board in a vibrant shade with Devnagari letters in gold proclaiming this to be the '*Mahakaleshwar Swayam Sahayata Group, Gudiya Aadivasi Paramparagat Veshbhusha me*', or the Mahakaleshwar Self-Help Group, specialists in traditional Bhil costume doll-making. Below the institution's name are the names of Ramesh and Shanti, both prefixed with the honorific 'Padma Shri' before their names.

Shanti warmly acknowledges my visit from Bengaluru as we step into a snug living space dominated by a wood-framed sofa with elegant fabric upholstery. The room is generously populated with a vast collection of dolls that immediately command attention. The figurines, appearing mostly as characters in pairs, are a colourful tribute to the Bhil tradition. Female figures, in vibrant attire are adorned with intricately formed miniature metal jewellery, some in elegant dance poses playing dandiya, others carrying firewood or baskets; while the male dolls, in flamboyant dhoti–kurta and turban, animatedly play drums slung around the neck or wielding bows and arrows. Each figurine narrates tales of *vanvasi* and *gramvasi* folk that dominate the rural Indian landscape of the region, crafted with life-infusing tenderness and meticulous artistry. In between this display, the remaining spaces on the walls are taken up by neatly framed commendation certificates, each narrating the craft and community work for which Ramesh and Shanti are renowned.

Their grandson, Arjun, offers me a glass of water and takes it back once I'm done. I commend him with a gentle pat on the head. His young mother, the daughter-in-law of the house, is draped in a saree with her head covered, exemplifying reverence for elders. She joins in the conversation, as if to explain her little boy's actions. 'The men in the family have always been independent but readily come forward to help with household chores. So, the younger ones have naturally picked up similar values.'

Ramesh calls Arjun over to his side while mentioning that the lad has also been eagerly waiting for our meeting. Pointing to the two distinctive cowlicks on the lad's head, he continues, 'The *jyotish* [astrologer] tells us that these are signs of impending greatness.' Meanwhile, the toddler granddaughter, the younger of the Parmar's grandchildren, rests comfortably in her father's arm, observing the interactions with playful eyes.

My eyes are drawn to a shrine within the room's alcove with divine figures so familiar in Hindu households. A central deity stands out, with one hand gripping a sword, radiating *shakti* or strength. Noticing my intrigued gaze, Ramesh softly explains, 'She is Vihat Mata, our ancestral *kuldevi*, the clan deity.' Then, getting up, he walks over to the shrine, and, with profound reverence, he cradles the deity, telling us that his own hands have sculpted this sacred representation. In that moment, I feel deeply moved by the gesture and it dawns on me that Ramesh's dedication and reverence for the family's sacred symbol, expressed through his craft, is the same force that inspired his other creations.

The Parmars are from a community of Jhabua with a rich heritage in leather craftsmanship. Ramesh reminisces about his grandfather Ramji and father Raghunathji having worked for generations as artisans for the erstwhile royal houses of Holkar and Scindia. However, following independence, the loss of patronage, restrictions on hunting and the rise of industrialisation meant that many artisans had to leave behind their traditional crafts and move into new economic opportunities. The march of 'progress' is not unique to India: many a civilisation has seen the decay of ancestral arts and crafts.

In the early 1990s, amidst financial struggles, Ramesh, the eldest of Ramji's children, faced the challenge of balancing family commitments and continuing with his education. And so it was that a neighbour, District Commandment Officer Ranjit Singh Solanki, noticing Ramesh's athletic talent, helped the young man enter into the Home Guard service.

However, the low-ranking government role paid poorly, brought little by way of respect, and was mired with bureaucratic obstacles. Posted on the border area of Madhya Pradesh, Ramesh soon found that his integrity often clashed with low-level corruption. On occasion, he even faced peer pressure to falsify information and mistreat innocent members of communities whose voices against injustice were muffled by bureaucracy. Ramesh resisted many unethical demands, and an unwillingness to comply led to frequent transfers to high-crime areas. Reflecting on a particular incident, he recalls a police inspector's scornful remark, 'Who do you think you are, seizing goods worth lakhs?' Such encounters deeply affected him, casting shadows on his once unyielding confidence.

As if to move us away from these unpleasant recollections of the past, Shanti lightens the mood by saying that dinner is ready. As is customary in many Indian homes, we all sit down on the floor in the lotus position while Shanti and her daughter-in law arrange the plates. The sweet, aromatic smell of *daal–baati*, a regional delicacy of lentils and hard wheat bread, fills the room. We sit and eat a simple, nutritious meal, intertwining fingerfuls of food while sharing happy stories in the warm embrace of the Parmar family.

From a young age, Ramesh was drawn to the world of art. Despite the hurdles in his work as Home Guard, he found comfort and expression in crafts such as wood sculpting and *Pithora*, a highly regarded traditional folk art. Local handicraft training centres became Ramesh's refuge and at one such centre, a chance meeting with Shri Narayan Vyas, Assistant Director at Jila Hathkargha Vibhag, marked a turning point.

Narayan Vyas took the young Ramesh under his wings and encouraged him in his artistic endeavours. Ramesh recalls how Narayan emphasised, 'Art transforms lives, Ramesh. It forges a path to self-reliance that goes beyond simply creating beautiful artefacts. Your talents can be a beacon of opportunity, sparking change for others.' And thus, the mantra *art can make you self-reliant, be a job giver instead of a seeker* became a guiding revelation, transcending societal expectations. Vyas's words stirred a profound realisation that he possessed not just a gift but also the potential to make a transformative impact through mentorship of the community around him through art.

Meanwhile, Shanti, motivated by familial values, a passion to make a difference, and with encouragement from both Ramesh and her father-in-law Ramji, enrolled in a doll-making course in 1993 at a nearby training facility under a government-funded programme for disadvantaged communities. Shanti recalls those times and how Ramji, skilled in leather crafts, nudged her, 'Don't waste time confined to household chores, learn a craft, embrace an art.'

'He would happily babysit our first-born infant while I attended the course.' Shanti lets off a delightful titter as she shares this nugget of her journey.

'Some of Ramji's ideas and expertise in leather craft were implemented in crafting dolls from a basic structure to more human-like figurines,' Ramesh explains, his voice tinged with pride. The sweetness of the moment is palpable as we sit together relishing *churma*, a sweet typically served with *daal–baati*, bridging the years that have passed.

Intrigued by their collaboration, I ask, 'Shanti learnt doll-making first. How did you join in?'

The soft hum of the ceiling fan and the faint aroma of sandalwood incense feels apposite as Ramesh reminisces about the crossroads that he had faced all those years ago. 'Being a Home Guard felt like a huge weight of responsibility. Each day was a battle, not just fighting the system but struggling with my own yearning for something better,' he muses as he gazes into the distance.

The frequency of visits to the handicraft centre increased and Narayan Vyas's keen eye recognised Ramesh's latent talent. 'He saw what I hadn't realised fully,' Ramesh admits with a smile. 'Narayan ji believed that our traditional craft could be reimagined so that it could tell stories and capture hearts.'

Engaging with artisans broadened Ramesh's horizons and an intuitive connection to doll-making emerged while Shanti pursued her course and he absorbed the intricacies from her.

'1993 was a defining year for us,' Shanti chimes in.

Ramesh continues, 'It wasn't just leaving the Home Guards, it was us embracing a shared dream, one that Narayan ji had given us a glimpse of. The beginning of a new chapter.' The door to artistic exploration had swung wide open and though the journey was fraught with uncertainties, Ramesh marched forward with his mentor's words reverberating in his mind.

In the realm of doll-making, as with many craft-related activities, while many are enticed by the promise of training grants and stipends, the demands of artistic patience, rigour and the level of finesse expected mean that many would-be-practitioners take the easy route and succumb to the allure of a regular daily wage.

Ramesh, guided by foresight, sought a dignified path, stating, 'I didn't want Shanti to labour for others.' Shanti agreed, preferring home-based work. And so, inspired by Narayan Vyas, they found resonance in the idea that handicraft could bring not just economic sustenance but also dignity.

Despite financial challenges, the couple's creativity blossomed as they crafted dolls from old clothes and scraps. Their talent stood out and hardships, such as having to sleep in stalls with little to eat at artisan fairs, were no barrier to accolades, and the invitations to attend subsequent exhibitions continued to pour in. With backing from the District Development Council, the Parmars began exhibiting their work in Ujjain, Ratlam, and Indore, earning wide acclaim and appreciation.

'Sometimes some of our own family and friends pulled us down, saying who makes dolls for a living? Then self-doubt crept in, but the mocking simply made us resolute, raising our belief that we would prosper,' Shanti says with a smile. The couple prioritised their craft, often making tough choices between spending on home essentials and craft materials.

Surprised by their resilience, I inquire about what had kept them motivated.

Ramesh, with a passionate glint in his eyes, admits to phases of doubt. 'I questioned our path,' he says, 'but always held onto hope for a brighter future.'

To this, Shanti, her eyes shining with pride, adds, 'Seeing someone value our art made every effort worthwhile. One unforgettable moment was our exhibition for ISRO employees,' she recalls, emotion evident in her voice. 'We hesitated, unsure if our hand-made dolls would connect with the audience, but the response was overwhelming. The scientists crowded our stall and were captivated by the craft and suddenly our dolls were selling rapidly. It felt like a dream!'

Taking a deep breath, Shanti continues, 'By day's end, every doll was sold. To know that our creations adorn the homes of those brilliant minds felt surreal and fuelled our determination.'

Another turning point was when a minister, Narendra Tomar, current Speaker of the Madhya Pradesh Assembly, visited them in Bhopal during a fair. Soon after, recognising the Parmars' talent, they were enrolled as registered artisans. This led to even more invitations to exhibitions, followed by an influx of orders and awards of recognition.

With the surge in demand for their dolls, Ramesh and Shanti saw the need to scale up production. The latent talents of the Bhil, the largest community in Jhabua and the surrounding areas between the Mahi and Narmada rivers, thus became a natural focus. While Ramesh discerned the potential and possibilities, he was acutely aware of the immediacy of monetary reward through manual labour, which for many in the community seemed easier than mastering the intricacies of doll-making. Nevertheless, Ramesh remained resolute in his goals, for this venture held economic opportunities for local women.

Venturing into villages, Ramesh encountered both social and economic obstacles, but he persevered with tact and empathy. He recognised a unique dynamic in a community steeped in tradition: while men externally projected bravado, it was the women who held significant influence within the households. He learnt that women were valued for their robustness and physical strength and that, in a marriage, these women not only proved economically resourceful but played pivotal roles in decision-making, resource allocation, and maintaining family welfare, with some even guiding their equally formidable husbands, showcasing their profound role in keeping family and community together.

This understanding guided Ramesh's approach as he conducted inclusive village meetings and counselling sessions, prioritising women's voices and concerns so as to elicit support for his expansion venture. In the once notorious village of Umari, Ramesh even met with former criminals, persuading many to engage in handicrafts. Through participation in craftwork and attending exhibitions, many changed their outlook on being seen as valued. Realising that the key to unlocking community potential lay in recognising and respecting the roles and dynamics already present, Ramesh replicated this approach in subsequent engagements.

As Ramesh's stature grew, his role went beyond informing and educating to bridging the gap between officials and local communities. In this, he promoted schemes like *Ladli Behen Yojna* and *Pradhan Mantri Aavas Yojna*, which empowered local communities through economic means. Overcoming bureaucratic hurdles, Ramesh and Shanti utilised grassroots experience to facilitate dialogue that turned intentions into actions.

Though remote villages sometimes suffer bureaucratic indifference and neglect, beacons of light and positive change emerge to challenge the status quo. One such was Dileep Soni, an officer from Hast Shilp Ayukt Vibhag, an atypical bureaucrat posted in Jhabua possessing a zeal for positive change.

Ramesh continues the story. 'When my name was suggested to Dileep ji, he was sceptical. However, he agreed to accompany me to Pitol, a village that the winds of progress seemed to have bypassed. Here, we met Lilabai, a formidable woman whose ideas resonated with Dileep ji.'

'Ramesh bhai has come and met us, and the women here are already familiar with bamboo work,' she replied.

'With Dileep ji's enthusiasm, we registered a thousand women for craft skilling in just five days. They were trained in *baans shilp*, the art of bamboo craft, but the officer didn't stop there, he leveraged his position to secure financial aid through Khadi Gram Udyog Vibhag, to support the community.' Ramesh's genuine demeanour and tactful communication skills transcended barriers of fear and reputation.

Ramesh even forged a connection with the formidable Ramila Bai, once a notorious criminal, who many local men and even police often hesitated to approach. Understanding that good leadership has a positive domino effect. Ramesh continued to identify, guide, and mentor influential local figures, which led to others participating in fresh opportunities.

The establishment of self-help groups under Ramila Bai marked a pivotal shift and these groups became epicentres for skill enhancement, economic empowerment, and community cohesion. From crafting traditional jewellery to mastering jute work, these initiatives not only provided avenues for reliable family income but also a means to preserve, promote, and successfully market traditional arts and crafts within an ever-burgeoning hostile era of mass production. Shanti emerged as a catalyst among the women in local *baithaks*, bringing to light opportunities for personal betterment while maintaining family nurture and welfare.

Women actively took up the challenge and participated but, initially, the men looked on, only gradually absorbing the unfolding transformation. Over time, by leveraging government grants, a few men have ventured into livestock farming, rearing *Kadaknath*, a local chicken breed with the coveted Geographical Indication (GI) tag, which is only granted to especially unique products to designate geographical origin, thus further bolstering economic prospects and community independence. An application to have the Jhabua dolls designated with the GI tag registration has also been filed, which will bring greater prestige and market worth the initiative that the Parmars have worked so hard for. Meanwhile, Ramila Bai had been proposed for the Mahila Adyaksh, women's chair – a position that marks her evolving stature as a leader in the community.

Yet, amidst these efforts, a poignant realisation emerges: the disconnect between India's formal education system and grassroots realities. Bureaucrats, entrusted with the task of driving change, often grapple with intricacies of on-ground implementation. In contrast, Ramesh and Shanti, with their innate wisdom and understanding, have navigated these challenges with a blend of empathy and perseverance, highlighting the invaluable lessons that life itself often bestows.

Their partnership is a testimony to resilience and collaboration, glued together by a happy marriage. Born in a small village and without much formal education, Shanti has, without seeming effort, championed the greater cause for India's rural women. She has naturally grown into her role being equally at home as trainer and mentor to rural women, travelling to villages offering encouragement and support, as well as attending exhibitions to promote the art and craft of Jhabua dolls. With doll-making earnings, the Parmars have secured their children's futures and built a home. The husband and wife complement one another; she stitches, while he paints and innovates, and together they have not only built a thriving craft business but also created hundreds of jobs which have contributed to the wellbeing of the community. Their synergy and mutual support stand as pillars of contented affection, as they share in the joys of success.

Nestled on a small, cramped terrace, is their workshop where I am greeted by a vibrant display of dolls at various stages of creation. Ramesh, the artisan, showcases his resourcefulness by talking through the production stages. 'We start with rags, you know. Waste bits of fabric from tailors become the stuffing and attire for our dolls,' he explains with a proud smile. Over the years, the Parmars have evolved their process, introducing cost-effective and eco-friendly techniques.

In a corner, Shanti manages a small cooking stove under a *chajja* (ledge), multitasking as she cooks alongside doll-making. Operational challenges are evident, but their determination shines through. 'Space is a constraint, and weather, especially during the rains, demands extra caution,' Shanti adds.

Ramesh takes me through the intricate process of creating their best-selling papier mâché dolls. Two small tanks hold a mixture of old cardboard scrap, water and a natural gum called *dhavra gond*, to which Ramesh adds a local black soil, known as *khadia mitti*, for a smooth finish and durability.

Displaying his ingenuity, Ramesh continues, 'To make it economical, I craft moulds at home using cement. The *papier mâché* mix, after being soaked for days, is put into moulds to shape the dolls' bodies. We use cloth gauze and a layer of refined flour to get a smooth finish for the doll's face.'

For the limbs, Ramesh uses stencils to draw the arms and legs on cardboard. The skin-coloured fabric, cut by the skilled hands of local women is stitched and stuffed with cloth shreds. 'As our earnings grew, we sourced cloth from Dahod, Gujarat. It's more economical,' Shanti adds.

Local markets provide miniature accessories like bows, arrows, musical instruments, and wicker baskets. The final strokes, including the intricate facial features, are painted by Ramesh himself. The result: an inexpensive doll showcasing traditional regional culture, embodying the essence of reduce, reuse, recycle.

Ramesh and Shanti's commitment to their art is often hampered by infrastructural challenges. Despite the availability of vacant buildings, bureaucratic red tape means that securing space for training centres remains a daunting task. A prime example is the vacant 'Dileep Club' nearby, once envisioned as a folk-art museum but now a symbol of neglect and missed opportunities. Like many unfashionable towns around the world, it seems that Jhabua too suffers from an officialdom that shows little interest in its development. Fortunately, Omji Sharma, an educator and an old friend of the Parmars, has provided a temporary space adjacent to his school, which is used to craft larger, more sought-after dolls. Ramesh and Shanti are also introducing their art to students as part of the National Education Policy, which emphasises skill-centric learning across India and aligns perfectly with Ramesh's pledge: 'I dedicate my craft to society, to ensure its enduring legacy.'

The evening draws to a close, and it is time to bid farewell to the Parmar family whose genuine warmth and hospitality have left an indelible mark on me. As I am about to embark on my journey to the airport, Ramesh and Shanti present me with an exquisitely crafted dual-figurine doll. 'This is a memento of our shared journey,' Ramesh explains, smiling with radiant humility, as he hands over the little labour of love. Moved by their gesture, I feel even more strongly that these dolls symbolise more than just art, they embody the indomitable spirit of Ramesh and Shanti, and the profound positive impact the craft has made for the local community.

The pictures of the memory of the couple's attire at the inauguration, which I had seen before my visit came back to me: Ramesh in a classic turban, jacket, and dhoti, and Shanti in a vibrant skirt paired with a contrasting *odhni*, complemented by shimmering jewellery. Curiosity piqued, I ask, 'What is the story behind your distinctive outfits for the inauguration and the Padma Shri ceremony?'

Ramesh chimes in, 'It has been a conscious decision, you know. We were advised to dress "formally" for the events, to blend in, so to speak. But Shanti and I believe that our traditional attire is our identity, it's who we are. It represents our heritage, our struggles, and our triumphs. So, we decided to wear what truly resonates with our souls.'

Shanti nods in agreement, 'Even Modi ji, took notice of us, for our outfit. Always stay rooted, for it is our roots that give us strength and direction,' he said, as we touched his feet, and he in return, reciprocated the gesture.

Their presence at the handicraft exhibition, against the divine backdrop of the Mahakaleshwar Mandir, Ujjain, symbolises a harmonious blend of *shakti* and *sarjanatmakta* – strength and creativity: a partnership of shared challenges, dreams and triumphs.

Together, Ramesh and Shanti navigate the intricate dance of life, each complementing the other, much like the eternal cosmic dance of Shiva and Shakti.

6

A Tongue on Every Stone: The Life of K.K. Muhammed

Ramanujam S.R.

I was incredulous when I first saw pictures of Bateshwar near Gwalior. So many temples in a single compound! The place looked unreal. Surely these photographs were photoshopped! Even friends who had grown up near Bateshwar were astonished, for they had not heard of the place. This was understandable because Bateshwar had been in ruins for a long time, restored only around 20 years ago.

That photoshop-like imagery was in fact a reality and the work of one man, Padmashri K.K. Muhammed, retired Regional Director of the Archaeological Survey of India (ASI). Surely it required an authoritarian personality to get this done, especially in a region renowned for dacoity, I thought!

KK, as he is popularly known, turned out to be the opposite. When I first sought a meeting with him in 2019, he graciously invited me, a stranger at the time, to his home. Extremely soft-spoken and a keen listener, KK indulged my naïve questions on temple architecture and pointed to the right sources. He also let me browse through his library.

When I meet him again in 2023, KK enthusiastically browses through heritage quizzes that a group of friends have created and are publicly shared through a website. He offers his own ideas for further quizzes on archaeology and readily agrees to speak to likeminded groups with interests in temple architecture and even signs his autobiography for me.

KK's eyes light up when I tell him that my guru on temple architecture has written a comparison between Greek and Sanskrit literature. Immediately coming across as sensitive, engaging, attentive, measured, and patient, he talks in a tone that shows his care to communicate in a way that will carry people along, and this must be part of the reason he has managed to complete so many monumental renovations, such as Bateshwar. In every interaction, his eagerness to promote archaeology comes out strongly.

Bateshwar came later in Mr KK's colourful and varied career, being his penultimate project before retirement. He was born in 1952 in a poor Malayali family of daily wage earners in Koduvally near Kozhikode. His father operated a truck while his mother wanted KK to be a religious priest.

However, with his own initiative the young lad switched from a religious madrasa to a primary school offering a diverse curriculum. Here, KK's teachers were to change the course of his life. One of them, Mr Abubakar, vividly narrated tales from the Indian epics, Ramayana and Mahabharata, while Mr Ganghadaran took the school on various virtual tours of historical sites as far as the north of India. Ms Susan, teaching English, Mr Shashidharan, his philosophy teacher, and Mr Velayudham, all helped KK immerse himself in his studies and made him deeply conscious of indigenous culture and individual and social responsibility.

Possessing an inquiring mind, KK lapped up knowledge from books at the local library, which inspired him to pursue a study of history. Fascinated by the narrations of master Ganghadaran, his eyes were set on north Indian colleges. But KK's father wanted him to join a small contracting business he had just set up and there was also an opportunity to become an Arabic teacher. However, KK stuck to his passion and obtained admission to Aligarh Muslim University (AMU) in 1973.

Despite his eagerness to study history, KK was quickly disillusioned at AMU. Due to his political affiliations, he found himself constantly struggling with Irfan Habib's group in the history department, being rejected for a PhD programme and research scholarship in favour of less qualified candidates favoured by the establishment.

In an attempt to escape the Marxist stranglehold on AMU's history department, he switched to archaeology, obtaining admission to the archaeology postgraduate diploma programme with the Archaeological Survey of India (ASI) in 1976. He soon realised that archaeology suited his temper and found himself enjoying the classes that were held at various locations around the country. These sites, with their immense wealth of culture and heritage, proved to be his laboratory and training ground for a career in the field.

While still an ASI student, the young KK joined Prof. B.B. Lal in investigative excavations of the history of Ayodhya. That initial field experience was to shape KK's professional life and over the years has come to define his personality and popularity in the public's imagination.

Upon completing postgraduate studies with ASI, KK returned to AMU as a member of the Department of Archaeology. After a ten-year stint, KK went back to ASI where he spent the remaining twenty-four years, and the most eventful period of his career.

At ASI, KK's work took him across the length and breadth of India. His career became an incredible journey of adventure and discovery. He has dug and delved into the hearts of ordinary Indians though his work. His tour of duty has taken him from Agra to Chennai, Goa, Raipur and Bhopal and eventually to the ruins of Bateshwar, before retiring from his role as Regional Director at the New Delhi ASI office in 2012.

Discoveries at Fatehpur Sikri

KK's earliest and perhaps most dramatic achievement was at Fatehpur Sikri.

In the 1500s, Emperor Akbar had hosted a series of conferences of world religions and established what came to be known as Din-I-Ilahi at Fatehpur Sikri. The exact location of the *Ibadat Khana*, where the conferences took place, had long remained uncertain. Historians had suggested several possible sites. A traditional scholar suggested an unexcavated mound as a potential site.

Despite much scepticism from academics, KK felt that the scholar's proposal had merit and, while examining historical images of the area surrounding the mound, he stumbled upon a painting of the *Ibadat Khana* as depicted by a court painter of the time. He noticed a striking resemblance to the unexcavated mound that had been pointed out by the traditional scholar.

Convinced of the connection, KK proposed an excavation, which was approved by team leaders. Thus, from 1981 to 1983, the site was meticulously excavated, eventually revealing the *Ibadat Khana* in perfect alignment with the depiction in the original 16th-century painting.

This momentous discovery marked a significant milestone in KK's career. From here, KK would also go on to discover the location of the first Christian chapel in North India. The Christian fathers invited by Akbar for the conferences at the *Ibadat Khana* were housed near the palace and a chapel was built. KK pinpointed a potential location, and the chapel was fully excavated. The Archbishop of Agra confirmed this to be consistent with historical records. As I talked to him about the connections he had made between texts and archaeological reality, his eyes sparkled with joy. It was almost as if I was seeing him at the moment when he had made that first connection.

Standing Up for Right and Truth

Meanwhile, the Fatehpur Sikri discoveries raised KK's professional stature – which attracted trouble at AMU. With no ideological alignment to the Irfan Habib camp, he had already been demoted and even informally stopped from borrowing books from the university library. Despite being denied recognition and facing false accusations, KK stood strong. Refusing to recognise Prof. Habib's flawed scholarship, KK documented his unfair dealings.

However, the toxic climate at the university made it apparent that his career at AMU was stalled. In 1998, KK therefore joined the ASI, but even then the powers made his exit troublesome, denying him the option to return to his position at AMU. There was also an attempt to rescind his appointment at ASI. Perhaps as a concession to the AMU powers, ASI posted him to distant Chennai rather that to Agra, where KK could have continued with the work he had previously begun and which he would have preferred.

In Chennai, KK would face yet another test of his mettle. It was 1990 and the Ayodhya agitation was at its peak.

Back in the 1970s, when he had been part of Prof. B.B. Lal's Ayodhya excavation team, KK had found temple pillar bases in the excavated grounds around the mosque that matched those within the structure. KK knew then that there was a temple beneath the mosque.

And so he published a letter in the *Indian Express* on 15 December 1990,[1] attesting his findings and supporting the stand of a renowned bureaucrat–scholar, Iravatham Mahadevan, who had asked for a detailed excavation in Ayodhya. In doing this, KK placed himself in a vulnerable position with ASI as he was still in probationary period and public pronouncements of this sort went against service rules and could attract straightforward dismissal.

Senior ASI officers took KK to task and threatened immediate suspension, but KK stood his ground and told the officers, '*Swa dhare nidhanam sreya*', meaning, 'in fulfilment of one's dharma, even death is welcome'. Shri Mahadevan supported KK and reached out within the bureaucracy, and along with the help of well-wishers, the suspension was avoided and KK was instead transferred to Goa.

Archaeologist on Tour of India

KK's tryst with Fatehpur Sikri would follow him to Goa. Here, KK discovered the remains of the fathers who had visited *Ibadat Khana* and then been murdered upon their return to Goa. Thereafter, KK initiated a search for the remains of Queen Ketavan, the patron saint of Georgia, which had been carried to Goa. Although KK did not find the remains, his successors persisted, achieving success in 2005. The discovery and the permanent loan of part of the remains to Georgia fostered closer ties between India and Georgia.

As I soon realised, KK made connections with many people through his work. To accommodate a dam, a Kurdi village in Goa was to be submerged and the Kurdi Mahadev Temple transplanted to a new location. It had therefore been dismantled but reconstruction was pending. KK completed the reconstruction in eighteen months, bringing relief to the workers who had feared divine wrath. When I mentioned KK's connection to Kurdi, a friend who hailed from the submerged village recalled it with nostalgia. I have kayaked in the Salaulim reservoir and it gives me goose bumps to think that submerged under the water I was boating on the sacred land where once stood the temple that KK transplanted.

KK's work in Goa earned him a promotion and transfer to Patna where renovations under his leadership read like an archaeologist's dream – Kumarahar, Pataliputra, Kesariya stupa at Vaishali, Nalanda, and Vikramshila being the most notable. At Rajgir, KK also carried out rapid excavations to discover and save a stupa with Buddha's relics which, being in the path of a proposed railway line, would have been irreversibly damaged.

I was elated to learn that I had visited many of these places and KK smiled indulgently when I told him I had travelled by scooty to get there. He explained why Kumarahar was nothing but earth now, all the architectural remains having been damaged and vandalised. I mentioned that I had missed seeing the Rajgir stupa so, soon after, he emailed a write-up with details.

KK's next stop was Agra and controversy followed him there. He stood firmly against a proposed shopping complex in the heritage area between the Taj Mahal and the Agra fort. With the Supreme Court's intervention, construction on Chief Minister Mayawati's pet project was put on hold. During this episode, KK protected his team inviting the government to proceed against him instead if they so wished.

Further conservation and heritage-protective positions he took up in Agra invited political attention and so KK was transferred again, this time to Raipur. KK found himself in the newly created state of Chhattisgarh, without even an office or accommodation. Yet, KK and his team chalked out an impressive heritage strategy for the State and helped ASI acquire valuable heritage land before the land prices shot up. Under his leadership, ASI adopted an unusual approach by actively urging citizens to explore their heritage. One means of doing this was via unconventional hoardings publicising historical sites such as Sirpur, Barsur and Malhar. KK also successfully communicated with Dantewada Naxalites, assuring them that ASI's work was benefiting local labourers with fair wages and thereby drawing them in to become facilitators of ASI work.

Relocating from Raipur to Bhopal, KK then renovated the Bhojeshwar Mandir, a grand Shiva temple that had been left incomplete. The open roof exposed the temple to the elements, causing structural damage. ASI ingeniously crafted a fibreglass roof with intricate carvings, addressing engineering concerns while seamlessly blending with the existing structure. In Amarkantak, faced with a budget shortfall for land acquisition, KK creatively persuaded a public sector unit to transfer pending dues to the district collector, which enabled ASI to acquire land, remove encroachments and renovate a heritage temple complex, bringing delight to all involved.

In his final posting in Delhi, KK played a pivotal role in preparing monuments for the 2010 Commonwealth Games. Despite working in dense and congested localities, ASI renovated forty-five monuments and reclaimed forty acres of encroached land. ASI also established a children's museum at Siri Fort, where KK pursued his passion, commissioning a collection of replicas of famous sculptures under one roof. Students from Bihar created 35 fibreglass replicas of grand sculptures from across the country. One of these is the *Tala Shiva* located near Bilaspur, an extraordinary sculpture without parallel. KK was delighted when I mentioned that I had seen the original on my visit to Bilaspur.

The Bateshwar Story

Among all their achievements, KK and his team mark the restoration of Bateshwar, Madhya Pradesh, as their greatest. The site, featuring two hundred miniature temples built by the Gujjar kings in the 8th to 11th centuries, lay scattered in ruins when KK and his team turned their attention to it. After seeking advice from an intelligence officer experienced in bringing local dacoits to justice, KK engaged with the notorious dacoit, Lachu Singh, outlining his plans and good intentions for Bateshwar. KK also made use of the connections that a few of his newly recruited local team had with some of the dacoits in order to build trust. During our conversation, KK recollects that Bateshwar was desolate, unlike anything he had seen anywhere else before. He recalled Jaswant Singh Gujjar, a team member, gesturing toward a Hanuman *murti* (idol) in one of the shrines among the ruins and saying that the dacoits worshipped here and proudly acknowledged that he too had been with them.

This is the same Jaswant Singh who was instrumental in helping me to meet KK. On my visit to Bateshwar, Jaswant Singh noticed that I was taking unusually long, slowly poring over the site, awestruck by the restoration. He brought out an album of 'Before' and 'After' pictures of Bateshwar expressing how proud he was to have worked with **KK**. Through him, I managed to reach **KK** for my first meeting with the archaeologist in 2019.

The process of raising the temples in Bateshwar demanded extensive technical attention and the refined instincts of an archaeologist. KK vividly recalls encountering a temple that defied identification; neither the deity nor the wall carvings provided any clues. KK observed an empty rectangular slot at the front that suggested a placeholder for Nandi, making it a Shiva *mandir* (temple). The team searched the site and located the *linga*, which fitted perfectly when placed in the shrine. Then, during *a pradakshina*, KK noticed a Nandi lying on the ground, seeming to gaze at him longingly. The Nandi fittingly occupied the vacant rectangular slot, perfectly completing the *mandir*, and Shiva and Nandi were reunited once again.

One day, on encountering a man smoking within a temple, **KK** admonished him, later discovering that he was the feared dacoit Nirbhay Singh Gujjar. **KK** conveyed to Nirbhay that he was a descendant of Gujjar kings and therefore should carry forward the work of his ancestors. The dacoit, delighted at his legacy and touched by KK's recitation of *Devi Mahatmayam*, turned to spirituality. Sadly, however, not long after, Gujjar died in a police encounter.

Mineral prospecting attracted the mining lobby, threatening the site and temples. Dismayed by government apathy, KK wrote a letter to the Rashtriya Swayamsevak Sangh chief, requesting his intervention in the Bharatiya Janata Party (BJP)-ruled state. This unprecedented act garnered public and media attention and forced the state government to restrain the mining lobby. Despite complaints from higher authorities, criticising KK's actions, no suspension followed, thanks to KK's well-wishers and his record of integrity.

Delhi and After

In his final posting in Delhi, KK created opportunities to fulfil his social responsibilities. Along with his wife, Rubaiya Muhammed, KK established five 'canvas' schools dedicated to educating the children of cross-state ASI labourers living and working far from their usual homes. The initiative gained momentum and noteworthy acknowledgement came in 2010 when former US President Barrack Obama and his wife Michelle Obama visited one of these schools. In 2015, when Obama visited India again, he wished to reconnect with a boy named Vishal, whom he had met on the earlier visit. Vishal, the son of a migrant worker, was located and found to be studying at St Columbus. This reunion between Obama and Vishal was a personally satisfying experience for KK. Reflecting on this effort, KK remembered that his childhood teacher, Mr Velayudham, who had instilled in him a sense of social responsibility, would have been content and fulfilled.

KK oozes passion and enthusiasm. He speaks excitedly about the Children's Museum, the replicas and his myriad ideas for a Sanskriti boat ride, a Shiva Museum in Varanasi and an ambitious dream of having replicas of all Asian artefacts housed under one roof in India. With a childlike glee, he showcased a small stupa containing sand from Buddhist sites, envisioning it as a highly collectable artefact bearing the authentic stamp of the ASI that could be crafted for 500 rupees and sold for 10,000 rupees. He has even drafted a picture book on Bateshwar, aimed at sharing its exciting story with children. On one occasion during a phone call, upon mentioning that I was planning to visit the prehistoric Edakkal caves in Kerala, I could hear the happiness in his voice.

His eyes sparkled when I expressed my intention, and he said, 'Archaeology is the art of putting a tongue to every stone.'

He has made so many stones, some standing, some in ruins and some buried, speak a beautiful language to so many of us.

Anyone pursuing a career in ASI has access to the most precious monuments in India and the opportunity to contribute to their discovery, renovation, and popularisation. What sets KK apart is his commitment to truth and determination to go the extra mile to get the work done. Then there is the question of why he dedicated time to the renovation of countless temples. Only he can answer that and his response is poignant.

When he was posted in Raipur, the Lafagarh Shiva temple's priest implored KK to rehabilitate the temple as it faced imminent collapse. KK could not, as he lacked funds and experienced staff in the fledgling Raipur office. KK states that he received a divine command from Lord Shiva in a dream that night. 'Muhammed, my temple is falling down, go and save it. I will do the needful.' The next day, KK received the additional charge of Bhopal, which gave him greater financial resources. KK says that Shiva was the one who provided the means, funds, staff, and jurisdiction – to enable the temple's renovation. KK initiated the renovation with a personal contribution.

KK is forthright in acknowledging the unique role he has as a Muslim archaeologist, saying, 'My ancestors wantonly destroyed several Hindu temples and Buddhist viharas, and I have been provided with an opportunity to repent for past sins.' Nalanda, Vikramshila, Sanchi, Amarkantak, Bateshwar, Bhojpur, and several other sites are the result of 'this inner atonement – *prayaschitta* – which were an all-consuming motivating force'.

On Ayodhya, just before the Supreme Court's final judgment was due in 2019, and well after KK had retired from ASI, the resolution of the dispute would once more lean on his conviction and integrity.

Some prominent historians, motivated by an ideological position that consistently raised objections to everything indigenous, even going to the extent of fabricating lies as history, had branded the excavation leader, Mr Mani, as 'communalist'. Suspecting that these Marxist historians were attempting to tarnish ASI's 2003 Ayodhya excavation report, KK felt he had to share facts that were as yet unknown in the public domain. He thus wrote in the *Times of India* reiterating the findings from Prof. B.B. Lal's excavations of 1976–77.[2] He also made another startling revelation: the 2003 ASI excavation team included four Muslim archaeologists and therefore there was no question of any 'communal' bias in the report. This revelation had the cathartic effect of nullifying Marxist propaganda against the ASI report.

KK was an obvious invitee to Ayodhya on 22 January 2024 but, on medical advice, was unable to attend. However, he was endlessly interviewed by media in the run up to the *prana pratishtha*. So, although not physically present in Ayodhya on the day, in celebrating Ram Lalla's homecoming, the nation saw this diligent, gentle, and honest man quietly offering a glimpse of *maryaada* – dignity – Shri Ram's own *darshan* bestowed upon one of the best among humans. Maryada Purushottam Ram had truly returned to Ayodhya.

As I was making my way out after a blissful *darshan* in Ayodhya, I received a WhatsApp message from KK. It was a collage of personalities who were instrumental in the reconstruction of Ram Mandir. KK's photo was right in the middle, surrounded by many cultural, religious, and political leaders and lawyers. Some had brought their intellectual heft to the struggle, others had fought using the legal route, and many more morally. In my mind, I pictured the media quizzing KK, 'What are you doing standing with all of these people?' I heard his response too in my mind. 'I stand for dharma, not with anyone.'

It is very likely that every day countless curious travellers – *yaatris* with a yearning to connect with the past – walk with wonder within some monument or site that has been discovered and rehabilitated by Padma Shri K.K. Muhammed. In these moments, they may recall the dedicated efforts that KK and his ASI colleagues have invested in preserving, protecting, promoting, and sharing this precious heritage with the public.

Padma Shri K.K. Muhammed's commitment to truth, his unflinching readiness to take the hard road, and willingness to go the extra mile have been crucial in preserving and protecting India's rich culture. His *prayaschitta* have given to us the gift of history and heritage. It behoves every Indian to continue the legacy on behalf of coming generations.

7

Kapil Kapoor: An Acharya in the Indian Knowledge Tradition

Avatans Kumar

'All men are intellectuals, but not all men have in society the function of intellectuals'

—Antonio Gramsci

When Antonio Gramsci uses the term 'intellectual' in his famous *Prison Notebooks* he considers all men to have the potential to be intellectual because all can use the innately available faculty of intellect. However, not all are intellectuals. Julian Brenda describes intellectuals as a tiny band of super-gifted and morally endowed philosopher–kings who constitute the conscience of mankind. Prof. Kapil Kapoor is one such intellectual.

It was a cold Thursday morning of 25 January 2023. As I sunk in my chair at work in a far northwest suburb of Chicago, I took my phone out of my pocket and put it on my desk. Suddenly, a WhatsApp notification popped on my lock screen. It was from one of the Jawaharlal Nehru University (JNU) alum groups I am a member of.

The message read: Prof. Kapil Kapoor gets Padma Bhushan. I jumped off my chair and pumped my fist in the air as my colleagues looked on, confused. 'Finally,' I whispered to myself.

Padma Bhushan is a rare honour and one of the highest civilian awards from the Government of the Republic of Bharat.

The Acharya

From Panini to Patanjali, Bhartrihari, Bhaskaracharya, Chanakya, Aryabhatta, Shankaracharya, Ramanujacharya, Madhava, Sri Aurobindo, and Swami Vivekananda, the Indian knowledge has an unbroken tradition of *rishis* and *acharyas* spanning thousands of years. Many in the Indian Knowledge Tradition (IKT) dedicated their endeavours in defence of dharma. Kapoor Sa'b (Sir) is an intellectual giant in this tradition.

In his famous 1967 essay, 'The Responsibility of Intellectuals', Chomsky ascribes three primary responsibilities of intellectuals. First, intellectuals are supposed to speak the truth and expose lies. Second, Chomsky argued that 'if it is the responsibility of the intellectual to insist upon the truth, it is also his duty to see events in their historical perspective'. Finally, he suggests that the intellectual should lift the veil of ideology, which is the underlying framework of ideas that limits the boundaries of debate.

Even a cursory look at his personal and professional life proves beyond doubt that Prof. Kapoor fits perfectly into the Chomskian framework of intellectuals. His pursuit of truth and his exposure of the lies and misconceptions proliferated by Indologists, Orientalists and Marxists are extraordinary. During the colonial era, 'outsiders' gained agency in describing Indian texts and traditions. Many even believed that Indians lacked access to the 'true' meaning of their own texts and traditions and also propagated the notion that Indians had never developed 'critical' and 'scientific' thinking; and hence, Indian texts should not be read in the way that Indians read and make meaning from them.

Through his efforts in the classroom as well as by means of his books and articles, his talks and seminars, Prof. Kapoor has consistently challenged these notions and, over time, has become instrumental in reversing much misinformation and many misconceptions about Indian culture and IKT.

Moreover, Prof. Kapoor is also an intellectual immersed head-to-toe in the Indic tradition. He possesses all four *lakshanas*, the characteristics that a scholar of repute is expected to possess in the IKT – *rishi, sanyasin, shishta*, and *parivrajaka*.

As a *rishi*, Prof. Kapoor has masterfully taught several graduate-level courses in IKT and mentored countless students who have, over the years, gone ahead to become IKT scholars in their own right. In the numerous books that Prof. Kapoor has written, he has provided commentaries on several original Indian texts that inform both scholars and lay public alike. Among his achievements in this area are his *Dimensions of Panini Grammar* and the highly regarded 11-volume *Encyclopaedia of Hinduism*, both of which exemplify his intellectual prowess. The impact of these works continues to inspire both contemporary scholars and society at large.

As a *sanyasin*, Prof. Kapoor is an exemplar steeped in the highest reaches of this uniquely Indic tradition, living a simple life utterly detached from worldly desires and prejudices while remaining connected to society through his work, even maintaining simplicity in his attire and living in a modest home throughout most of his teaching career. He has also consistently stayed away from glitzy seminars and avoided the messy business of research grants that might compromise the academic integrity of his lifework.

In his discourse and interactions with people, Prof. Kapoor maintains *shishta*, being one of the politest, cultured, and kind-hearted individuals, never known to use harsh language, even against his fiercest critics. One of his professional mentors was Prof. Namvar Singh, a Marxist literary critic and academic, with whom, despite their ideological differences, he shared a special rapport and maintained a close bond over many years. Prof. Kapoor's sagacity and generosity are well known, for I have found that he is most gracious in obliging to speak and share knowledge at conferences and talks.

As a *parivrajaka*, Kapoor Sa'b is immensely satisfied with what he has. True to the IKS tradition, he maintains the highest level of academic integrity, not writing grant proposals that go against these principles or seeking to punch tickets to foreign conferences.

Intellectual *Kshatriya*

Dharma is the core of Hindu society. It is the universal principle that upholds the cosmological balance. It is benevolent and propounded to secure all living beings' good. The Mahabharata defines dharma in the following manner:

- Dharma is so called because it sustains and upholds individuals and community; hence, whatever sustains is dharma.
- Dharma is propounded to secure the good of all living beings; hence, whatever fulfils that aim is dharma.

- What comes from love for all beings is dharma. This is the criterion to judge dharma from adharma.

The *Prithvi Sukta* (14.1 and 14.2) of the *Atharva Veda* (roughly 12th century BCE) offers an exciting insight into the inner workings of the Hindu dharma.

यो नो द्वेषत्पृथिवी यः पृतन्याद्योऽभिदासान्मनसा यो वधेन ।
तं नो भूमे रन्धय पूर्वकृत्वरि ॥१४ ॥

O' Mother Earth, subdue those, as you have always done, who hate us, attack us, strike us, or mentally consider us their enemies || 14

The mantra calls upon Mother Earth to subdue those threatening us with 'mind – शास्त्र [śāstra] and weapons – शस्त्र [śastra]'. Simply put, the mantra calls for the defence of dharma on two fronts – at the intellectual level and on the battlefield.

Prof. Kapoor was, for much of his academic career, an academic at JNU in New Delhi, serving as professor at the Centre for Linguistics and English and also as Pro-Vice Chancellor, before retiring in 2005.

The culturally hostile environment at JNU meant that Prof. Kapoor had to frequently stand up to opponents of the Indic tradition and speak out in defence of dharma. Despite encountering numerous stumbling blocks, Prof. Kapoor was instrumental in setting up the Centre for Sanskrit Studies and, later, the School of Sanskrit and Indic Studies at JNU.

The ideological opposition that Prof. Kapoor and others continue to face in institutions like JNU stems from the effects of social engineering narratives and projects that have come to define post-colonial India, at the core of which is opposition to anything indigenous,

Hindu, or sanatana dharma, euphemistically referred to as 'majoritarian'. This opposition has been deliberately extended to Sanskrit, simply as a result of the language's association with Hinduism. As Prof. Kapoor has written in his *Introduction to Sanskrit Studies*, Vol. 1 (Special Centre for Sanskrit Studies, Jawaharlal Nehru University, New Delhi): 'This mindset required not just the exclusion of "Sanskrit Culture" but a positive opposition to it.'

Besides Hindi and English, the JNU School of Languages has long boasted a dozen or so foreign language centres. However, it was not until 2002, during Prof. Kapoor's tenure as Pro-Vice Chancellor and well over three decades after the founding through an Act of Indian parliament of JNU as a publicly funded research university, that the Special Centre for Sanskrit Studies was established.

Among many stumbling blocks was the objection to the design of the building for the newly announced Centre, whose proposed profile was shaped in the ancient cultural symbol of *Swastika*, sacred to Hindus and Jains, as a befitting representation of the Centre for Sanskrit Studies. While opponents of the design called it 'majoritarian' and 'communal', Prof. Kapoor argued that *Swastika* – well-being, auspiciousness – also belonged to Jains, a micro-minority community indigenous to India, and successfully fended off the ideologically motivated opposition.

As part of the design, the building included lighting on the rooftop which, as Prof. Kapoor explained during an interview, had been designed so that the Centre would be a visible landmark from the air, come day or night; the JNU campus being close to Delhi's international airport, night-time flyers would be sure to see the auspicious *Swastika* lighting up the building.

The Indian Knowledge Tradition

India is a knowledge-based civilisation, being one of the longest and also arguably one of the most advanced, unbroken cultural traditions of its kind – a tradition that has contributed invaluable philosophical wisdom, such as in the Vedas and Upanishads, to humankind.

Besides this, the IKT has made immense contributions in many other fields of intellectual inquiry. For example, physician Sushruta described rhinoplasty surgery in 600 BCE in his book *Sushruta Samhita*. Similarly, according to the Fields Medallist mathematician Manjul Bhargava, the so-called Pythagorean theorem was first documented about 800 BCE in Bauddhayana's *Shulba Sutra*, centuries before the Greeks.

The West is at last recognising that Indian mathematicians had mastered the concepts of what today is known as Algebra. Following in Bauddhayana's and others' footsteps from before the common era, Indian mathematicians developed the critically important decimal place value system, notation for zero and a logical definition of negative numbers.

These foundations enabled Bhaskaracharya, Aryabhatta (c. 5th century CE), Brahmagupta (c. 6th century CE), and later Mahaviracharya (c. 9th century CE), to formulate and apply algorithms and then to formulate and solve problems hundreds of years before these ideas came to be known and accepted in Europe. Indeed, the term 'algorithm' which has come to define these fundamentals of computation, was coined by Europeans, and is associated with Al Khwarizmi, a Persian polymath from the Aral Sea region who was a leading scholar of the 9th century CE Arab school in Baghdad.

Al Khwarizmi borrowed from and acknowledged the immense influence of Indian mathematicians in his works. Not only did Al Khwarizmi use translations of Indian classics such as the *Siddhanta* on the motion of planets which had earlier been brought to the Middle East by Ujjain scholars, but he also translated the Indian method of calculation as contained in *Hisab-i-Hind* by which the methods passed to Europe. We know now that the roots of Calculus lie in India and are considered to have spread to the West through the Kerala School of Mathematics.

The IKT is also a tradition of great argumentation and disputation, where the study of language – *bhasha* – reigned supreme. Vedic scholars – grammarians and philosophers alike – believed that a universe of objective realities exists because they can be expressed through human language. According to Bhartrihari, all language unpacks all knowledge. His ज्ञानम् सर्वम् शब्देन भाषते can be considered akin to 'I speak therefore I am'.

Three of the six *Vedangas*, the prerequisites to learning the Vedas – *shiksha* (phonetics), *vyakaran* (grammar), and *nirukt* (etymology) – are also directly related to the study of language.

The Professor

Prof. Kapoor is part of the Indic intellectual lineage that has given us scholars like Panini, Patanjali, Yaska, and Bhartihari, and today is considered one of the foremost *archaryas* in the tradition.

Born in Amritsar, Punjab, in November 1940, the precocious Kapil was destined to be a scholar despite not being fond of the regimen of school. When their father took the young Kapil and his sister who was two and a half years older, to enrol in the local primary school, the teacher asked Kapoor Sa'b which grade he wished to enrol in. Kapoor Sa'b, wanting to be with his sister, said, 'Fifth grade'.

One of Prof. Kapoor's childhood English teachers, perhaps in 6th or 7th grade, was Shri Brahmanandaji. Prof. Kapoor said he learned the essence of 'generative grammar' from Shri Brahmanandaji. Prof. Kapoor's teaching style – probing and immersive class participation – draws heavily from Brahmanandaji.

Generative grammar is a linguistic theory that transformed the field of linguistics in the modern era. In his monograph *Syntactic Structures* (1957), American linguist Noam Chomsky popularised transformational generative grammar. This 'grammar' draws its inspiration from Sanskrit Grammarian Panini's work *Ashtadhyayi* (6th–4th century BCE).

Prof. Kapoor comes from a family of educators. All three of his uncles from his mother's side were professors, one of whom was a philosopher. He once told Prof. Kapoor that there are only two classes of humans: good and not good. That made a profound impression on a young Kapil Kapoor's impressionable mind. He decided to be on the 'good' side of humanity, a decision he has endeavoured to live with for the rest of his life.

Prof. Kapoor progressed rapidly through his formal education and received his master's degree at nineteen, while still a teenager. He taught and mentored scores of scholars before formally retiring from his Pro-Vice Chancellor role at JNU. However, a scholar like Prof. Kapoor never retires from the intellectual life. Over the years, he has continued to lecture at various international platforms such as the House of Lords in the UK Parliament, where he spoke on Society and Polity in India. Within India, in the true tradition as *Guru*, Prof. Kapoor continues to support scholarship in IKS and has graced several INDICA events for which he has received the 'Grateful to Gurus' citation. Besides being Editor-in-Chief of the *Encyclopaedia of Hinduism* (2012) and the Sahitya Akademi-sponsored *Encyclopaedia of Indian Poetics* (2022), Prof. Kapoor is also the chairman of the Indian Institute of Advanced Studies, Shimla, to which he was appointed in 2018.

Prof. Kapoor is fondly known as Kapoor Sa'b among his students. I had the great privilege of learning from Kapoor Sa'b and first learnt of him in 1990 upon joining JNU's MPhil degree programme in Linguistics at the Centre for Linguistics and English. My seniors encouraged me to sign on to his lectures on the Indian Grammatical Tradition (IGT), which inspired me on the path of self-exploration of India's storied intellectual past. At the time that Kapoor Sa'b first began teaching IGT as a subject at JNU, it was the only such course offered by an Indian university. Prof. Kapoor also broke new ground by introducing courses in Indian poetics and Natyashastra, which were truly 'radical' in an environment that had largely neglected the worth of indigenous knowledge.

Later on in my studies, I also learnt the art and science of research from Prof. Kapoor's lectures on Research Methodology. Prof. Kapoor's classes were so prized that they commonly came to be respectfully known as *pravachan* – sermon, intellectual discourse – among his students. Even when presenting dry topics such as research methodology, Prof. Kapoor maintained a lively, engaging, easy, and fun approach that we always looked forward to. I still have the handwritten research paper I wrote on *Yaskacharya's Nirukt*, which Prof. Kapoor mentioned in his letter of recommendation for my admission to the graduate programme in Linguistics at the University of Illinois.

Kapoor Sa'b epitomises India's *katha-pravachan parampara* – story and discourse tradition – in Punjabiaccented Hindi and English infused with his vibrant personality making his courses inspiring, intellectually fulfilling, and fun. Our department was located on the first floor of the School of Languages building. 'We would know the moment Kapoor Saheb entered the building,' reminisced Surendra Rawat, a retired administrative officer of the Centre for Linguistics and English. 'His loud laughter was like the sound alarm of his entry into the building.'

Kapoor Sa'b has a great sense of humour for which he credits his father, saying, 'You see, my father used to call himself Lord Kapoor,' he once told us. His father was a landlord in undivided pre-Independence Punjab. Upon partition, his father would say the land stayed behind in what became the Islamic Republic of Pakistan, but the 'Lord' had to come over to the Indian side.

'My intelligence is from my mom,' says Kapoor Sa'b. 'My mother taught me everything, and she knew everything,' recounts Prof. Kapoor. She taught him Urdu, Sanskrit, and Mathematics.

The day the Padma awards were announced, I called up Kapoor Sa'b. He was delighted and excited. 'It is a recognition of the [Indian Knowledge] Tradition,' he told me.

A recognition indeed. A long-overdue one.

8

S. Ramakrishnan:
Finding Purpose in *Seva*

Aparna M. Sridhar

Back in the 1960s and 1970s, the fervour of post-Independence times meant that, for many a young man, joining the armed forces after an engineering degree was the dream. This was no less true in the Tamil Nadu hinterland where parents encouraged their sons either to go to the big cities in India or make careers in the national services, paving the way for themselves in a new India.

And so S. Ramakrishnan from Ayikudy, a small, pretty village nestled amongst hills and fields in the south of Tamil Nadu, came to Bangalore (now Bengaluru) for an Indian Navy selection interview. This was a huge move for the young man, for he had hopes of a life serving the nation at sea, leaving behind the tranquillity of his rural upbringing close to the famous Kutralam and the Agasthiyar falls in Tenkasi district in an area of natural beauty so vividly captured in the song '*Chinna Chinna Aasai*' or '*Dil Hai Chhota Ssa*' from the movie *Roja*.

Fate, however, had other plans. On 10 January 1975, during the selection process, Ramakrishnan's life changed forever. He was just about to complete the fourth and final year of his engineering degree and had entered the field with high hopes, but on this day he met with a tragic accident, causing serious injuries to his spine. He has remained wheelchair-bound ever since.

This life-altering accident crushed the dreams of the tall handsome young man in the prime of his youth. Yet, even to this day, Ramakrishnan is philosophical and phlegmatic. In his clear and resonant voice, he quotes a Tamil saying, *'Kuttu pattalum mothira kaiyala kuttu padanum'* – 'Even a knock on one's head must be from someone wearing a ring on his hand.'

Such a serious injury not only meant suffering the tragedy of disability, but the cost of treatment and care would have been prohibitive for most families. However, since the accident occurred during a selection process for the armed services, the Indian Ministry of Defence took full care of Ramakrishnan.

Traumatised and confused, Ramakrishnan was hospitalised at Command Hospital Air Force, near Cambridge Layout in Bangalore where, as the only spinal injury patient, he remained bedridden for four months, after which he was moved to Pune for rehabilitation. There he was one of eighty patients from around the country and stayed for another sixteen months.

On being discharged, Ramakrishnan returned to his spartan home in Ayikudy where his distraught parents tried desperately to create a new life for their young son. To give him a sense of privacy and independence, they even put up a thatched shed on the ground opposite the main house. That household, like many across India, followed the popular Sanskrit *Subashitam*, which declares that 'the very purpose of life is to lead a life of purpose':

Paropakaaramvahantinadya, paropakaaramduhantigaaya |
Paropakaaramphalantivriksha, paropakaaramidamshariram | |

'Just as rivers flow for the benefit of others, cows give milk for the benefit of others, trees bear fruit for the benefit of others, so it is that the human body is meant for the service of others.'

The first four years after the accident were spent sleeping and recovering, but somewhere in the recesses of his mind, Ramakrishnan knew that he had to bounce back. Friends would come by for conversations and the odd game of chess to cheer him up. In the mornings and evenings, Ramakrishnan would summon up the will and tutor his own siblings and the children of neighbours in mathematics and science in their preparations for school examinations.

The year 1981, six years after the accident, was a watershed year for Ramakrishnan. Possessing a transistor that kept him company, he was an avid listener of All India Radio broadcasts from local Tirunelveli and Chennai stations as well as Radio Ceylon. It was the International Year for the Disabled and there was much news coverage of events along with many dramas and speeches that both offered information to all and sundry and motivated the disabled. Listening to these programmes helped Ramakrishnan connect with the world outside. 'I used to wonder if I could ever do anything,' says Ramakrishnan, 'and providentially, in 1981, I was inspired by these broadcasts, and so we started Amar Seva Sangam.'

His doctor and later mentor, Air Marshal Dr Amarjit Singh Chahal, was the inspiration for the name of the organisation. The affable doctor had been accredited with developing the first Spinal Cord Injury Centre for the armed forces. Later, Dr Amarjit set up a paraplegic home in Pune in 1974, the first of its kind in India. To this day, Ramakrishnan draws inspiration from Dr Amarjit's pioneering work and, so motivated, continues to serve the differently abled in his own way.

Extremely well-read but also spiritually assured in his dharmic roots, Ramakrishnan follows the words that Swami Vivekananda articulated at Rameshwaram over a century ago – '*Shiv Bhave Jiv Seva* and *Daridra Narayana*' – equating service to the needy is service to the divine.

Based in Ayikudy, Amar Seva Sangam has changed the lives of the disabled not only directly through the therapeutic and support services provided but also through path-breaking institutional and legal changes.

Amar Seva Sangam was formally registered as a charitable institution in 1985, following which, Sivasankari, a well-known journalist, wrote an article in the popular Tamil weekly *Ananda Vikatan* about Ramakrishnan. This article led to a spate of interest and, as a result, Amar Seva Sangam received several complimentary letters of goodwill along with financial contributions. One of the journal's readers, Sulochana Srinivasan from Mumbai, whose husband at that time worked in Allahabad Bank, even helped raise funds. She introduced Ramakrishnan and Amar Seva Sangam to the Jindal Trust that began sending 8,000 rupees every six months, a substantial amount in those times.

Speaking of those early days, Ramakrishnan says, 'With the initial funds, we bought an old house, and we also started a library, which we called "Writer Sivasankari Library" in honour of the journalist who helped us get the initial publicity. Then we developed the school little by little.'

Ramakrishnan, despite limited mobility, has always been very particular about striking a personal rapport with people. He has travelled far and wide and takes time to speak to people, describing the nature of the work of Amar Seva Sangam. His visible persistence and total negation of his own discomfort has been an inspiration to the people he meets, and his infectious enthusiasm motivates many to help in the cause.

Later on, other publications like *Dinarmalar* interviewed him, and so word about Amar Seva Sangam spread even wider. Soon, Siva Saraswathi Vidyalaya, which had begun as a primary school housed in a thatched shed with just five students, a lone teacher on a salary of 60 rupees and a maid on 20 rupees, had grown into a Higher Secondary school with scores of children.

In 1985, Ramakrishnan met his biggest ally and soon to be his wife and partner in Amar Seva Sangam. At the time, Lakshmi, who Ramakrishnan affectionately calls Chitra, was singing a *Ganapati krithi*. Ramakrishnan was struck by Lakshmi's simplicity and gentle manner. She accepted Ramakrishnan's proposal, recognising that he needed a soul mate to develop the Sangam further. Today, Lakshmi remains at the heart of Amar Seva Sangam, showering love on all the children that are in their care.

Meanwhile, Ramakrishnan remained acutely aware that his dreams were lofty, yet his means humble. Born and raised in a deeply dharmic family, he turned to the highest and most revered *aharyas* (highly learned persons or teachers) of sanatana dharma, whose blessings he knew would be his guide. These enlightened *acharyas* represent *mathas* (Hindu institute or college usually affiliated with a Hindu temple), some of which have traditions that stretch over 2000 years and, even today, remain relevant as beacons that preserve and promote the spiritual wisdom of Bharat. Ramakrishnan mentions the blessings of Parmacharya of Kanchi Kamakoti Peetham, which are seen by many as divine prophecy. On the guidance of Sringeri Acharya, Ramakrishnan performed *Devi Parayanam* (incantation of all the Devis names) for 48 days, which he believes infused energy – *shakti* – to his life's cause.

Over the course of time, Ramakrishnan has visited and collaborated with several institutions that support the disabled, including the Socio Economic Education Development Society (SEEDS), which is India's leading integrated Corporate Social Responsibility and Social Intervention implementing agency.

Further articles in national newspapers, such as the *Indian Express*, have resulted in many joining Amar Seva Sangam as volunteers. Ramakrishnan has remained committed to reach out and enjoin all who share his vision of inclusivity and compassion for the differently abled to support the organisation's work. To this end, he has gathered a small group of dedicated individuals, each with their own set of skills and experiences, and formed a strong team. The path has not been easy; scepticism, financial hurdles and logistical nightmares have all been obstacles that this man, who must depend on others for his mobility, has had to face and overcome.

In 1990, Ramakrishnan went to Madras (now Chennai), on a fundraising mission and stayed at an aunt's home for three months, with the family arranging for a driver to take him around the city during his campaign. His first visit was to meet famous Carnatic singer and Bharat Ratna recipient, the late M.S. Subbalakshmi. Initially, Subbalakshmi Amma's secretary refused to offer an appointment, stating that the singer, being elderly, could not meet visitors, but upon seeing Ramakrishnan being lifted into the car, he was called back and granted a meeting.

Sadasivam Mama, Subbalakshmi Amma's husband, helped with fundraising, something that he had done for several charities through his wife's soulful music. And so it was that Subbalakshmi Amma sang at IIT Madras's cultural programme 'Mardi Gras' as well as at the Yeluru Gupta Foundation to raise funds for Amar Seva Sangam. The philanthropic couple also introduced Ramakrishnan to two of India's largest conglomerates, Tata and Birla.

In Subbalakshmi Amma, Ramakrishnan had found a gem: a true Bharat Ratna. Immersed in spirituality, Subbalakshmi Amma had raised and donated generously to various charities throughout her life. Among many high-profile institutions, she has helped raise funds to support the work of Tirumala Tirupati Devasthanam in Vedic scholarship and other organisations supporting the physically challenged. That Subbalakshmi Amma supported these causes, generously offering her time and talent, inspired Ramakrishnan immensely.

Not long after, another fundraising concert by vocalist Maharajapuram Santhanam was arranged at Narada Gana Sabha in Madras. Among the many who attended were the parents of Sankar Raman, a chartered accountant and social entrepreneur with muscular dystrophy.

Young and dynamic, Sankar Raman left a lucrative private practice and came to Ayikudy to join Amar Seva Sangam and is now its chief functionary. Bringing his financial and business acumen, yet steeped in the ethics and values of the organisation that Ramakrishnan had set up, Sankar Raman set about the task of organising Amar Seva Sangam into a world class charity institution. Among the changes that have been institutionalised include sound operational and financial management and transparent and seamless systems to account for donations from India and abroad.

Never averse to meeting people, Ramakrishnan once went to see film director K. Balachander while the latter was in town for a shoot. Being occupied with commitments, he asked Ramakrishnan to meet his assistant director, who had directed the film *Sigaram*. Speaking about that meeting, Ramakrishnan says, 'We met the assistant director Anandu and told him our story. That interaction prompted the making of a film, *Vaaname Ellai*, a story of how five people contemplating suicide are inspired to change course upon seeing a disabled person lead a life of dignity. My life history made a deep impact on him.'

Word of Ramakrishnan's work was well known and so it was natural that connections with the Indian Navy would ensue. Meeting Admiral Ramdas, the Chief of Naval Staff in Chennai, paved the way for a formal association between Amar Seva Sangam and the naval unit INS Kattabomman in Tirunelveli. The naval connection continues, with Ramakrishnan visiting INS Adyar in Chennai in 2023.

From small beginnings under a thatched roof 40 years ago, Amar Seva Sangam has expanded and today the site occupies 32 acres, with some parts yet to be developed.

After the growth of the school for children with disabilities, 1991 saw the inauguration of an integrated school, where children with disabilities could be educated alongside their able-bodied colleagues in six classrooms.

Alongside schooling, a dormitory shelter was also constructed. Also in 1991, its first year of operation, nearly 60 polio camps were held. In this, the Rotary Club of Kutralam enabled Amar Seva Sangam to connect with medical specialists in polio management. This enabled the Sangam to conduct polio detection camps and provide support to the afflicted by making available wheelchairs, callipers, crutches, and other appliances to enable mobility and independence. In partnership with the local Aravind Hospital, eye camps were also organised, enabling treatment for curable conditions like cataracts.

The concept of *dhanam* permeates life as lived by the ordinary Indian, and both individuals and institutions are inclined to contribute to the wellbeing of one's community and social welfare. Even large charitable organisations came forward not just to support Amar Seva Sangam monetarily but also with offers of manpower and donations of equipment. In one case, simply as a consequence of affiliation with Ayikudy to his *kuladaivam* family deity,

Lord Balasubramanyam Swamy, a bank official, donated 9.5 lakh rupees for the purchase of an ambulance.

It is heartening to see that both individuals and corporations are often driven by strong social values. As the leader of Rashtriya Swayamsevak Sangh, Shri Mohan Bhagwat has said in 2023, 'What we call "*seva*", service, is deeply rooted in our society. It predates the modern concept of Corporate Social Responsibility, as our outlook on *seva* is that there is no expectation of anything in return for it.' The essence and truth of this idea keeps recurring again and again in Ramakrishnan's story.

Ramakrishnan not only wanted to establish a centre that would support the differently abled, but he also wanted to ensure their inclusion and integration in society. Throughout this journey, he maintained contact with Dr Amarjit, both while the latter was with the Indian Peace Keeping Force and later as the Director General of Air Force Medical Services. He and Major H.P.S. Ahluwalia came to Ayikudy in 1995–96 and conducted a paraplegics workshop funded by the Indian Spinal Injuries Centre, which Dr Amarjit had founded along with the major after his retirement from the air force.

In 1995, Amar Seva Sangam was part of a historic programme titled 'Law and the Disabled' at Ayikudy, carried out under the guidance of Justice V.R. Krishna Iyer, which led to a multi-organisational push for change. This initiative resulted in the Indian parliament passing the Persons with Disability (PWD) Act in December that year. This ground-breaking Act brought about a radical change in the approach to social welfare, with a focus on safety measures and prevention, the early detection of disabilities and the empowerment, education and employment of persons with disability. This law has changed the lives of many, granting rights and benefits that support living with dignity.

Nearly half a century after his accident, Ramakrishnan is still always seen with the mark of *vibhuti* (sacred ash) on his forehead. Now approaching seventy, Ramakrishnan lives each moment in keeping with his late guru Krishna Premi's words: '*Sukham dukham laabam nashtam arohyam roham idhukkum bhagavannukkum sambandham kidayadhu*' – 'There is no connection between our life experiences and the Supreme.' Expressing his way in words, Ramakrishnan says simply, 'What Bhagavan [God] gives us is devotion to him, we need to surrender totally.'

Ramakrishnan is content watching his young wards develop, grow, and learn to be independent, working as diligent students and pursuing further education; flying away from the nest but often returning to Amar Seva Sangam as visitors and volunteers. While his own health sees ups and downs, Ramakrishnan exudes an aura of contentment, a soul deeply fulfilled with the part he has played in bringing together a dedicated team of workers to nurture the children in his care and to seek the best possible resources for Amar Seva Sangam.

Sitting in his chair speaking into the phone held up by a stand, his loud clear voice ends with a promise to keep in touch. Having met him every summer at the Brindavan Temple in nearby Ambasamudram, one is reminded of the words of Kanchi Paramacharya, who said, 'In the miracles of a few great men we can see a vision of the divine.'

The dust and heat settle on a hot day, and the river Thamirabarani gently flows along its course, serving all in its course.

9

The Mother of Mother Trees: Tulsi Gowda

Mythili Rao

I've been invited by Tulsi Gowda to take a mid-morning walk in the mini forest that surrounds her rural coastal north Karnataka home.

The fresh air is punctuated by the sound of birds and insects. Tulsi is gently touching a plant here, caressing a leaf there, looking up to the trees as if silently talking to them, asking them about their wellbeing, like a mother would to her children. Accompanying us is her grandson, Santosh, who remarks that when she walks, she does not look at the ground but around, ahead and up at the trees. It is as if she is surveying her treasured grove of green.

In 2020, an entire nation looked on as this frail-looking but immensely strong lady walked up the aisle of the Durbar Hall at Rashtrapati Bhavan with ease and simplicity – wrapped in a traditional sari, simple jewellery around her neck and wrists, and hair tied in a bun – to receive the Padma Shri from President Ram Nath Kovind. Her feet, seasoned for decades walking bare shod on the forest floor, seemed to sink into the thick carpet of Rashtrapati Bhavan. The question in the minds of curious onlookers must surely have been, 'Where on earth had she been hiding and how did we miss her all these years?'

The enormity of the moment was significant, for Tulsi Gowda is only the second person from the Halakki Vokkalu community to receive this honour, bringing national recognition and respect for the strong matriarchal values that hold families and culture together in India's Vanvasi communities.

To members of the Halakki Vokkalu and the Forestry Department alike she is a '*vruksha devata*' or goddess of trees; for environmentalists she is a human 'encyclopaedia of the forest'; while, to the young among her community, she is simply Tulsi *Ajji* or Tulsi Granny.

For this octogenarian environmentalist, born into a Halakki family in Honnalli village in Uttara Kannada District of Karnataka, age is just a number. Retirement from a formal governmental position has in no way diminished her passion for preserving nature that has defined her entire life.

Being born in poverty, the lack of formal schooling and loss of her father while she was just two years old were no barriers for young Tulsi. She grew up and ventured into a life full of discovery and adventure while remaining rooted in her Vanvasi forest traditions.

To help support the family, Tulsi joined her mother when she was barely fourteen and began working in the Forestry Department's Agasur nursery. Here, surrounded by trees, she began her practical education from Vanvasi elders who had been bequeathed traditional forest knowledge handed down by generations. The sharp eye of now retired forest officer and researcher Shri Yellappa Reddy was quick to spot Tulsi's ability to absorb knowledge and develop unique skills, as well as her general keenness and curiosity, and so he gave her opportunities to progress in the Forestry

Department. After all, the forest was her home and the trees she was now helping to cultivate in the nursery were her children.

In those early days, nobody could have imagined that Tulsi's work in the nursery would change the destiny of the forest and the land that it occupied. Soon, through her knowledge of the soil, of plant and tree varieties, and by nurturing tens of thousands of saplings, if not more, at Agasur over the course of decades, Tulsi became a force to be reckoned with in the Forestry Department's reforestation efforts in Honnalli and surrounding areas. Her care, commitment, and sheer love for the trees she cultivated as saplings, have over the years proved to be instrumental in the reforestation of the Mastikatta range of Uttara Kannada, Karnataka.

From the very beginning, Tulsi had an affinity for the environment; her innate passion for nature and her interest in the wellbeing and interdependence of flora and fauna motivated her to acquire knowledge of the dynamics of their survival. The forest became her de facto school as she grew to understand the factors causing environment degradation, such as the increasing urbanisation of rural communities and the ill-effects of deforestation and destruction of habitat on humans, fauna and other flora. It is *anubhava* (experience) of the ecology of her native forest environment that has made Tulsi what she is.

In keeping with Vanvasi tradition, Tulsi married early. Her husband, Govinde Gowda, though much older than Tulsi, did not deter her from pursuing her passion as she continued her work in forestry. Tulsi bore him two children, a boy and a girl, and despite losing her husband when she was in her fifties, Tulsi, now a grandmother of three, has led a rich and varied family and social life.

Over the years working in the forest, walking barefoot and seeking out the 'Mother Tree' of every species, noting the location and then taking responsibility for each step of plant regeneration – from harvesting seeds, incubating and ensuring germination and growth of the tender saplings and then planting them in the forest – became the hallmark of Tulsi's role with the Forestry Department. Her experientially developed knowledge of native plants enabled her to nurture them in their journey from nursery to forest.

As we walk, we chat about Tulsi's time in the forest. She patiently explains the complete process that is followed in the successful exercise from identification of the seed to germinating it and then transferring a viable sapling onto the forest floor.

Continuing, she tells me, 'It is God's gift that I have been granted a keen sense of observation from having lived with the trees my entire life. Trees bloom and seeds germinate. But there is a skill and a right time to collect the seeds; a right time to germinate them. The Mother Tree offers itself, but there can be neither haste nor delay. Nature works in its own time.'

Tulsi elaborates further, saying, 'We are aware that the highest knowledge in this universe is experiential and not theoretical. It is the same here in the forest.'

I ask Tulsi whether there is a method to what she has been doing all these years and, if so, has she taught this to anyone or has it been documented. She remains silent, her twinkling eyes and well-weathered face radiating a gentle smile. After some moments, Santosh fills the silence, explaining that this cannot be done because, though Tulsi *Ajji* 'knows' all of this, she cannot explain the 'how'. 'It is an intuitive process which cannot be verbalised. To do this one has to let her walk in the forest being free to do what she has done for sixty years nurturing trees and follow her every step to record the entire process.' However, when experts have tried to do this, *Ajji* has been unable to do anything, saying that she feels too self-conscious and that being watched distracts her.

Santosh went on, 'When *Ajji* is in the forest, she forgets everything else.' It is as if he is speaking of a person who has fallen deeply into a transcendental state of devotion that takes them onto a different plane. '*Ajji* does not need GPS to track the path and find her way; it is as if the trees are leading her. In fact, she has never worn any footwear and feels most comfortable walking barefoot.'

Santosh recounted other incidents from *Ajji*'s eventful life in the forest. 'In the forest, she is totally fearless walking about alone even while aware that it is home to some dangerous wild animals. *Ajji* has had many a close encounter with king cobra, tiger, and even the elusive leopard in her regular forest forays. In fact, *Ajji* told me of a close encounter with a tiger. She just folded her hands, offered some *prarthana* [prayer], and the big beast simply walked away.' From such stories, legends are born.

Forestry Department records, as well as other sources, suggest that Tulsi has planted around one lakh (100,000) trees! However, during our conversation, Santosh explained that *Ajji*'s work covered five forestry plantations and she planted nearly ten thousand saplings each year in each of them. She began when she was fourteen, so even if we took the time of her retirement to be sixty (though in reality she continued to work long after that), the numbers would be incredible. Looking at this amazing woman, it is not difficult to imagine that she has indeed planted entire forests.

Among her achievements, Tulsi has identified the seeds, germinated and nurtured the saplings, and successfully planted over three hundred medicinal plant varieties, of which knowledge has been passed on in a continuing tradition with many still used to treat common ailments by village folk.

A strong believer in the power of education, Tulsi has worked to promote environmental education and traditional ecology practices at all levels, from primary school to university. Even in her advancing years, she is invited to address students in schools and colleges. She joyfully explains that she never misses such opportunities and feels honoured to share knowledge. 'Children should be encouraged to look after the seed and the plant. I explain to them the importance of and the need for forests.' It is inspiring that Tulsi has been able to impart to students her immense practical experience of the environment, the ecology of forests and the role that humankind needs to play in shaping a sustainable future for all flora and fauna.

Tulsi's activities have not been limited to raising and planting trees. She has consistently taken a stand on environmental matters and sustainable development. In 1980 she joined public protests in opposition to a hydroelectric power project on the Western Ghats. While such projects may be motivated by the drive for economic and social progress – with an emphasis on developing much-needed utilities, providing employment, and improving living standards – they can also have adverse, long-term, and sometimes even irreversible negative impacts.

Tulsi *Ajji* raised her voice about the devastating effects of this particular proposal that included the submergence of huge areas of forest and the loss of scores of villages whose populations would have had to be relocated and rehoused, not to mention permanent loss of habitat for many endangered plant and animal species. The combined efforts by all involved proved successful and the proposal was abandoned.

Going beyond her day job as sapling propagator and tree planter, Tulsi has for decades worked with like-minded people on forest conservation and anti-poaching initiatives, reducing the incidence of forest fires, preserving biodiversity and water resources, and promoting organic farming. Through her work Tulsi has also been both an inspiration to women and an advocate for gender equality and Vanvasi rights.

Utilising her considerable knowledge, Tulsi has trained scores of local people toward ecological behaviour with natural resources such as water harvesting and soil conservation. Tulsi worries that the rains are not as regular as in former times, with unpredictable variation from one season to the next being common. She remembers that a decade ago, the stream near her home would burst its banks so much during the monsoon that villagers were cut off from the main road. Tulsi played a role in getting a bridge constructed to alleviate the situation.

Tulsi also understands the folly of planting acacia and eucalyptus trees and the long-term negative environmental repercussions of these species. She has advised the authorities about this but to little avail, with the result that forest areas bursting with these water-table-depleting species hinder the growth of native species that are so vital for eco-conservation.

Agasur Honnalli is about 20 km from the town of Ankola in coastal north Karnataka. Being far from the cosmopolitan cities of Bengaluru and Mysore, the area typifies the real India, where rural and urban merge seamlessly and traditions still define lifestyle. As the car navigated the pot-holed road, we suddenly came upon a sign showing directions to Tulsi Gowda's home, indicating her popularity.

When I ask her about her fame locally, she tells me that, because of the signage, she has had many a tourist and passer-by drop in to meet her. Tulsi remains unflustered by such impromptu visits, saying that they give her more opportunities to talk about trees and the forest and raise wider consciousness about the importance of preserving and nurturing the environment.

Tulsi's work has been recognised for long. Prior to the Padma Shri, she had received various accolades. She talked of receiving the Indira Priyadarshini Vriksh Mitra Award in 1986 and recalled her meeting with Maneka Gandhi in New Delhi. The award, as its name indicates ('Vriksh Mitra' means friend of trees), was recognition for her contributions towards enhancing the growth of forests and tree cover. Even on that occasion, she raised the matter of the ill-effects of acacia and eucalyptus tree planting, which the government was then actively promoting as a strategy for increasing forest cover. Among more than a dozen awards that have been conferred on Tulsi is the Kannada Rajyotsava Award, which she received in 1999. And the awards kept coming. In June 2023, the University of Agricultural Sciences, Dharwad, awarded Tulsi an honorary doctorate, which was followed by the 'Champions of Change Karnataka' award for her contribution to social welfare by the Interactive Forum on Indian Economy.

Despite the many public accolades, there is a sense of discontent and disappointment in the family. Apparently, records related to Tulsi's years of service with the Forestry Department, referred to as the muster roll, have been lost, depriving her of the due rightful pension.

Tulsi tells me that the Forestry Department recommended her for the Padma Shri and even encouraged her to go in person to the conferment ceremony at Rashtrapati Bhavan. While she is gracious about the recognition she has received through the Padma, Tulsi is clear that work on preserving and protecting the environment is far more important than any award. Nothing takes precedence over nurturing saplings, planting trees, and saving forests. The trophies and citations occupy the sitting room of Tulsi's simple home, neatly displayed in glass cabinets made specifically for that purpose.

Tulsi showed me the Padma medallion, her warm smile displaying a pride filled with humility and reverence. It felt a privilege to be in the presence of such an unassuming yet extraordinary woman whose experiential forest education aced anything one might learn in a conventional college. Being allowed to hold the Padma Shri and seeing the citation scroll were the highlights of my visit.

As a means of carrying Tulsi's legacy forward, the family is considering setting up a Trust as well as a nursery and a forest school to widen access to and awareness of conservation and reforestation.

'*Ajji* is slowly losing her memory nowadays,' said Santosh.

It is depressing to think that the knowledge Tulsi has accumulated over the long years may be lost the day we lose her. No concerted attempt seems to have been made to document it. When speaking to Tulsi it feels as if this knowledge resides deep within her, at an unconscious level. Perhaps such knowledge cannot be formally learnt, it must come through the accumulated *karma* of numerous births. Perhaps this knowledge is a divine gift, quite unlike something that can be gained through reading hundreds of books or spending years in a laboratory. Perhaps even the best training may need some prior intuitive gifts and innate abilities in order to bear fruit. However one might speculate on these matters, it is clear that Tulsi is a classic example of one who has grown up within, imbibed and then utilised indigenous knowledge and love of nature in the cause of protecting biodiversity and combating climate change.

Like other Vanvasi communities, Tulsi's Halakki folk have a strong matriarchal family structure where women are endowed with the responsibility of the nurturing of children, family, and community as well as nature. Through her eventful life, Tulsi has held these values close to her heart and her long association with the Forestry Department has led her to achieve extraordinarily impactful results, not just with reforestation and raising community consciousness of the environment but also in cherishing and promoting deep-rooted cultural heritage.

As we come to the end of our meeting, Tulsi makes a humble submission about knowledge. 'I don't know how I know! I just know,' she said. 'We need forests. Without forests, there is no water, no crops, the sun becomes unbearably hot. If forests thrive, the people and the nation will too.'

10

Sindhutai Sapkal: Mother of Thousands

Aniya Burse

During her eventful lifetime, the late Sindhutai Sapkal, who passed away in January 2022, had become known by many titles; but 'Mai', 'The Mother of Orphans', is her defining legacy and continues to mark this real Padma – a true lotus – out for her work with children.

It is almost impossible not to admire Sindhutai when one listens to her speeches. Mai's demeanour, tone of voice and mannerisms all give the impression of a compassionate, seasoned woman, schooled in life, rising to become a social reformer who positively impacted the lives of thousands. As I learned more about her, I found that this schooling was far from conventional. The confidence radiating from her voice came from experiences that would have worn down many, but which built her up and made her what she became. Hardship led Sindhutai to the path of becoming Mai – Mother – leaving a lasting legacy of caring for people in need.

Sindhutai was born in November 1948 into a family of simple cow herders in Pimpri, Meghe, a small village in rural Maharashtra. Affectionately named Chindhi or rag by her mother, Sindhutai spent her childhood caring for their small herd of cows, which provided a meagre livelihood for the family. Her father, Abhimanyu Sathe, had seen a spark in his daughter and, against her mother's wishes, encouraged her to pursue an education. However, Sindhutai's formal schooling only lasted four years; in her words, she was a 'half-time, fourth-grade pass-out'.

Sindhutai left school and not long after married Shrihari Sapkal, a man in his thirties, and began married life in Navargaon forest. At the tender age of twelve, Sindhutai had become responsible for all household duties, with little support from her husband.

The little ray of light that Sindhutai held inside of her seemed to be fizzling out. However, one thing in her life still sparked joy: reading. She would save newspaper pages reused to wrap groceries, collecting them to read the news, poems, and stories. She savoured the words; each passage felt like a morsel that ought to last forever. This precious spark of joy became scarcer as the years progressed, for Shrihari did not allow her to read. Being uneducated and unable to read himself, he saw Sindhutai's only source of happiness as an act of disrespect, thinking that it could not be possible that his wife, still a child, was more intelligent than him. To comfort his ego, he would burn her poems; however, being at the age of rebellious behaviour, Sindhutai refused to give up reading. She would hide her precious papers under mattresses, furniture, in fact, any place she could think of. Sindhutai resorted to hiding her poems in the holes in the walls. Unfortunately, the rats found them and often chewed through the paper, leaving her with nothing to read again. Sometimes, in desperation, she would memorise the text and then swallow the paper, washing it down with a glass of water. Much later in life, Sindhutai recalled those memories, recounting that the poems she had scavenged and swallowed in childhood began flowing out, mesmerising audiences wherever she went.

While still in her teens, Sindhutai bore three sons to add to her never-ending domestic responsibilities. Apart from household duties, she also took part in helping the village with local affairs and grew into an outspoken woman. Even while pregnant with her fourth child, Sindhutai fought for herself and fellow small-scale farmers who needed help, speaking up for them and fighting for fair compensation from the forestry department in return for cow dung biofuel.

Her outspokenness angered the local collector, who spread rumours of Sindhutai's infidelity around her village. Enraged and humiliated, her husband beat his nine-month-pregnant wife unconscious and left her in their cow shed surrounded by animals as mute spectators. A cow gently stood over Sindhutai as she gave birth to a daughter, Mamta. For what seemed too long, the infant was silent. Sindhutai, still half-conscious, grabbed a stone and struck the umbilical cord, her eyes clamping shut as she counted each hit before she was finally able to free and embrace her daughter, who began crying after the sixteenth strike.

As if in a gesture of thanks, Sindhutai flung one arm around the cow that had stood over her. 'Mai, I hope to embody you. Today, I vow to help those who can offer nothing. I will strive to help others just as you have helped me.' A few days later, once she had regained her strength, Sindhutai fled the shed to escape ostracization.

Sindhutai first ran to her mother but, fearing the shame Sindhutai might bring upon the family, she rejected Sindhutai and her supposedly illegitimate granddaughter. So, the young mother and her infant had to resort to begging at train stations just to survive. At those times, Sindhutai thought to herself that if only her father had still been alive things would have turned out differently.

Sindhutai hopped from one platform to another, seeking out kind passengers on their way to their destinations, singing *bhajans* and *abhangas* (devotional songs and poetry) to earn whatever food the travellers offered in return for their generosity. She quickly learned that there were others just like her and realised that she was lucky to be alive.

Sindhutai also realised that she was now part of a community of homeless and began sharing her earnings with those around her. In return for providing them with food, the community would provide her with protection. But in the dead of night, while the rest slept, paranoia would catch up with her. She would run to nearby funeral grounds for shelter, which were quiet and empty. Here she would watch the remains of corpses smoulder as she hid in the shadows, waiting for the dust to settle. The settling dust allowed Sindhutai to satiate her hunger as she scavenged the dough ball *pind* (food) offerings laid out by the pyres and used them to cook her bare meals.

After a few months of living an exhausting life, she tried to end it all. She was desperate and felt that it was better to die than to continuously suffer. Mother and daughter would perish together, she thought. So, she scraped up her rations, made one last meal, and ate heartily before her death. But with every bite her yearning for death diminished.

She suddenly heard disquieting cries near her. A man was begging for someone to help him in his final moments. A voice inside her whispered, 'You are making a mistake, Sindhutai. Here is someone begging for help, and here you are thoughtlessly giving up on life. If you cannot live for yourself, live for others. Live for the ones that have nothing. Do not let your life go to waste.' With this thought, Sindhutai approached the man and fed him. The dying man was allowed another day of life because of her meal.

This small act gave her satisfaction and inspired her to live again – and so, in her words, she 'cancelled' her suicide.

However, getting back to normal life was not as feasible as one would think. Sindhutai faced hurdles and fell into the same depressing mental state many times. Her wanderings led her to Chikhaldara, a picturesque area of Amravati district, Maharashtra, where she once again attempted a failed suicide. Sindhutai had prepared to throw herself off a cliff, planning to leave little Mamta behind beside a tree; but before stepping off the cliff, she glanced back at Mamta and noticed something peculiar: many of the branches of the tree had been hacked off. She thought about the damaged tree and compared its state to her own situation. Sindhutai asked herself, 'If this tree can endure abuse and stand tall, why can't I?' Sindhutai 'cancelled' her suicide once again.

After this attempt, Sindhutai began to consciously seek out positive opportunities as a social worker, and her first such contact was with Vanvasi folk in remote parts of the surrounding area. Living around Chikhaldara led her to learn about a tiger preservation project that had displaced the local populations of over 80 villages and impounded 132 cows along with the death of one. She joined the villagers in their fight for rehabilitation and even confronted the Minister of Forests and petitioned the Prime Minister. The Vanvasi villagers took Sindhutai to their hearts, fed and housed her, giving her a true sense of belonging for what seemed like the very first time. Soon, Sindhutai felt it natural to identify herself with the community; she saw herself as a Vanvasi. These events were significant in Sindhutai's life.

Through them, she gained confidence, self-worth and an identity, becoming a human being of substance who could serve others. Sindhutai decided to stay in Chikhaldara to help the Vanvasis. However, she wanted her daughter to study in a place like Pune to cultivate her intelligence. Sindhutai had been prodding and discouraging herself from making this decision. Where in Pune would she go? How would she pay for the schooling? After a year, she finally decided to go to Pune for Mamta's sake. She was determined to provide a good education for her daughter.

Sindhutai wandered around Pune, getting an idea of where she would have Mamta stay. As she walked through the streets, she stumbled onto the Bal Gandharva Ranga Mandir. At the gate, she saw numerous billboards announcing an event regarding the friendship treaty between India and Russia. Sindhutai, aware of the importance of this event, decided to go inside. She was stopped by the guards but managed to convince them to let her inside. Sindhutai walked into the hall. The ceiling seemed to float above the officials. The guests on the dais delivered their speeches one after another. During a buffer period, Sindhutai rushed onto the stage and spoke her mind. She advocated for the help of the weak and to stand united to strengthen the nation. She finished her speech with a song:

> *Hamse na tu khane ki na pine ke baat kar, ees duniya me mardo ki tarha jeene ki baat kar.*
> *Jees Matrubhumi ki tu goad me pala, jees ki pavitra dhul me ghutno ke bal chala,*
> *Uske fate aanchal ko tu seene ki bat kar, mardo ki taraha jeene ki baat kar...*
> Speak not of indulgences of eating and drinking. Live life as a soldier fighting for the nation.
> Pay respects to the sacred land in whose lap we were born and raised.
> Put aside petty differences and work towards how we may all live together.

She touched the hearts of the audience who sat in awe as she sang. When she fell silent, the audience erupted into rounds of applause. Sindhutai stayed in the hall until the session ended, listening intently to the other speeches. During a recess, many speakers approached Sindhutai. They inquired about her background and her work. Two of these speakers were Ramprasad Pardeshi and Yashwant Kharat.

While conversing with Mr Pardeshi, Sindhutai said she had come to Pune for her daughter's schooling but did not have the necessary financial resources. Ramprasad Pardeshi offered his help by contacting Prataproa Godse, the president of the Shrimant Dagduseth Halwai Ganpati Trust. The Mandir's trust uses some of its funds for community welfare programmes like rural development, providing homes for the elderly and educating children from impoverished families. As expected, Prataproa Godse helped Mamta enrol in Sewasadan Girl's Hostel and covered all her yearly expenses. Sindhutai thus felt the weight on her shoulders lighten but her heart got heavier looking at Mamta. Sindhutai promised Mamta to take her home for holidays, embracing her in a tight hug before waving goodbye. Being a bright student, Mamta pursued her education and went on to receive a master's degree in social work.

Yashwant Kharat, the other person she met that day, was Director at All India Radio Station in Pune. Impressed with her voice, he invited her to the studios to sing for the radio. Later Sindhutai was asked for an interview, which led to her becoming famous with many getting to know her name. Thereafter, Sindhutai was invited to many institutions as a guest speaker. After learning more about her work for Vanvasis, many people wanted to help her with various forms of donations.

At the end of one such event in Pune, a woman with a young boy approached her. The woman introduced the boy as Deepak Gaikwad and asked Sindhutai if she would take him under her wing. During his childhood, Deepak struggled with frequent seizures, and the family had neither the resources nor the motivation to take care of him. Sindhutai understood Deepak's pain and loneliness, both of which were evident on his face. She was determined to make sure no one else went through the torture she was put through by being abandoned. Sindhutai accepted Deepak as a son with open arms. From this moment on, the mother-and-son duo came to be attached at the hip. He became an older brother to Mamta and all the siblings that were yet to come.

Sindhutai left Pune for the Adivasis in Melghat, Chikhaldara. It soon became a routine to travel to Pune for *bhajans* and then back to Chikhaldara with the funds raised at the events to help the Vanvasis.

It wasn't just Mamta who she left in Pune. She also gave up Chindhi and took on the name Sindhu, her favourite river and considered sacred by many. Adopting this new identity symbolised her purpose in life. Just like a river is the nourisher for surrounding life, Sindhutai could be the same for those around her.

She soon became continuously agitated by corrupt forest officers taking advantage of innocent Vanvasis. Sindhutai would not stand by as this injustice occurred. She had to take significant steps to force the deaf government to hear. Sindhutai went on a hunger strike outside the Tehsil office from 15 to 18 January 1985.

Observing Sindhutai's dedication, Vanvasis from eighty-six villages went on strike with her. Soon, news of the hunger strike made headlines in the newspapers. Government officials bore the brunt of public outrage and were forced to take cognisance and accept all the demands made by Sindhutai to end the hunger strike. Sindhutai's name spread even further, establishing her as a courageous activist. Prestigious institutions started awarding her and provided her with larger platforms to advocate for her mission. Sindhutai used the award money and the donations collected from such events to buy land to establish her organisations.

Sindhutai travelled across Maharashtra, making speeches and appealing for contributions from the public. She soon realised that conveying her message to a larger audience required another method: media. She put her story on paper, authoring a book titled *Me Vanvasi: I, Dweller of the Forest*. After several difficulties in publishing and distributing the book, Sindhutai initially managed to sell only a few copies, but as word spread, the book eventually became popular, and five editions were completely sold out.

Later, Sindhutai was invited to the Vishwa Marathi Sahitya Sammelan in 2009 in the USA, where she was able to promote her book on the international stage. While speaking at the event, she gave a powerful insight into the meaning of a woman. 'Every woman is a *Mai* – a mother,' she said. 'A woman's purpose is to nurture her loved ones and care for those around her. As the mothers of future generations, we are responsible for raising children with values that will build a healthy and productive society. We should forgive the ones who have hurt us and give them a chance to redeem themselves, just as you would do for your children.'

Throughout her entire life, Sindhutai has led by example, forgiving her husband for his wrongdoings, and even thanking him for the journey that led her to become Sindhutai. She took him into her ashram in his old age as if he were one of her children. She even cared for others while she was wandering, destitute and alone, filling the role of Mai, taking homeless children under her wings.

Today, Sindhutai's children, both biological (Mamata and Arun) and adopted (Deepak and others), together manage the four active organisations that she founded. Savitribai Phule Girls Hostel, Chikhaldara (founded in 1992), Mamta Bal Sadan, Saswad, Pune (1994), and Sanmati Bal Niketan at Manjri and Hadapsar (1995) are dedicated to the care of children, while the fourth organisation, the Gopika Gai Rakshan Kendra founded in 1998 at Wardha, set up and run as uniquely Indian Hindu tradition, is a refuge and haven for cows.

Unfortunately, the number of donors who support Sindhutai's organisations has decreased since her passing. This directly affects the wellbeing of children in the care of the organisations that bear her stamp. As Sindhutai always said, '*Bhasan nahi tar Rashan nahi*: I have won hundreds of awards, but they are all useless if I cannot care for my children. I give speeches to get the donations needed to feed my children. I could get all the recognition from the world, but it would be pointless if I could not satisfy their hunger.'

Today, her daughter Mamta encourages visitors to the ashrams founded by Sindhutai. 'Just stay with us for a couple of hours. We will all enjoy your company. It will be greatly appreciated if you decide to donate, but just spending your time with our children will be enough for us.'

During the course of her life, Sindhutai completely changed the destiny of scores of her adopted children. Over the decades, many of them have gone on to great achievements because of the support that Sindhutai's legacy offered them. Among these are professors, lawyers, and doctors. When asked about her experiences under Sindhutai's care, Neeti Sindhutai Sapkal said, 'Mai has taught me to live, fight, and help. Thanks to Mai's blessings, I can work as a nurse, and help others.' Another of Sindhutai's children, Deepali Sindhutai Sapkal wished to be reborn with Sindhutai as her mother, saying that even if she had known her biological mother, she couldn't compare with Sindhutai.

I walk away from Sindhutai's story with this poetic line *'Hamse na tu khane ki na pine ke baat kar, is duniya me mardo ki tarha jeene ki baat kar'* resonating in my mind. It encompasses the essence of Sindhutai Sapkal: an impoverished woman whose endurance, richness of heart and generosity of spirit rose and brought such joy and happiness to thousands.

Sindhutai's story is an inspiration. To discover and share her story is a privilege.

Thank you, Sindhutai.

11

The Fruit Seller's School: The Story of Harekala Hajabba

Ishaan Channa Reddy

Imagine for a moment that you are a street vendor at a bus stop when someone stops by and asks you about the cost of your products – except that you don't understand what they are saying.

That is where Shri Harekala Hajabba found himself in 1978 when an English-speaking tourist asked him for the price of his fruit. Hajabba was unable to answer, as he could only speak Tulu, a local language spoken in the coastal district of southern Karnataka.

'I am not an educated person,' he tells me in our meeting. 'But from that moment, I realised the value and importance of education.'

Shri Hajabba's lack of a formal education underlined a problem with schooling in many parts of the world, including India. Some small, remote villages simply did not have schools to which modest families on rural incomes could easily send their children. However, from that moment on, rather than wallowing in self-pity, Shri Hajabba decided to do something that was to help change the lives of hundreds to come.

Born in the late 1950s in Newpadupa, on the coast of Karnataka, Shri Harekala Hajabba grew up in poverty.

His father worked as a fisherman, only coming home once every eight days, and his mother worked long hours as a maidservant in other people's homes. These two largely absent adults were his role models growing up.

Fisher-folk families of the village lived in small, thatched-roof houses. Shri Hajabba's simple family home even lacked a door. They had no mats to sleep on and Shri Hajabba made do without a change of clothes.

'My days in the past were very difficult,' he tells us in our interview. 'Those first sixteen years of my life were very difficult,' he repeats, without any sense of regret.

While there was a school in the village, Shri Hajabba's parents simply couldn't afford to send him there. So, instead, the young boy would often go fishing in a nearby river, play with tamarind seeds and look for mangoes as a way of staying occupied.

In 1974, when Shri Hajabba was sixteen, he, along with his mother, little sister, and grandmother were forced to watch while their small house was washed away in a devastating flood. The place he had called home was gone in an instant.

With the home gone, and with few opportunities in the village, Shri Hajabba moved to Mangaluru in the hope of earning a living. In Mangaluru, the young lad took up selling oranges as a street vendor. But all that would change in 1978, on that fateful day when he was approached by an English-speaking tourist.

'I understood nothing when a man asked me in English the price of my oranges. I felt discomforted,' Hajabba told us. 'The man just moved away and asked some of the other vendors around me. This made me even more uncomfortable.'

The incident had left Hajabba humiliated. Arriving at the place he had made home in the city after a long day,

Shri Hajabba reflected on how he might ensure no one would suffer the feeling of incompetence like he had. And so, the very next day he approached a typist and told him of his plight. In those days, typists were very much in demand, especially by common folk who needed a professional writer to make applications and appeals on their behalf to local authorities. This typist agreed to prepare an application on behalf of Shri Hajabba making an appeal to the local Member of the Legislative Assembly (MLA) that a school be opened in the village of Newpadupa.

Shri Hajabba believed in the justice of his application request and he was excited. But after many weeks of waiting there was no sign of any progress. He therefore visited the MLA office in person but still failed to get any response. For weeks on end, he continued making frequent visits to enquire about his application, but each time he did he was told, 'We shall see what can be done.'

This pattern frustrated Shri Hajabba, as he recalled, when asked by a news reporter. 'After a few days, I understood that these people are just making me go round from one office to another. It cost me a lot of money and time. I therefore simply stopped going to my village to save time.'

Shri Hajabba decided to take matters into his own hands.

Over the next few years, he continued to sell oranges in Mangaluru, often sleeping in the bus stand and sometimes even going hungry, so as to save up money for the village school that he dreamed of. His commitment to convince the authorities remained firm as he continued to stand outside government offices for days with applications.

Many people praised him for his efforts. Others thought he was crazy. But Shri Hajabba continued. Finally, in June 2000, nearly twenty years after the tourist incident, a plot of land of around 1.33 acres was allotted to the school. It may have seemed like a success, but it was only the beginning.

While construction of the first buildings of the school got underway, Shri Hajabba contacted the management of the local madrasa, to ask if the new school could begin classes in one of their rooms. They gladly agreed, and so a class of twenty-eight students became the first to be taught there.

After years of construction, the first building was finally ready and, in 2004, classes one through five began to be taught in the school that Shri Hajabba had dreamed of. Besides saving up money for the project, Shri Hajabba would continue contacting various people and organisations, asking if they would lend money to his school.

'I got help from the District Commissioner Shivananda Murthy,' he told us in our interview. 'He even encouraged journalists to write about me. And so it was that "Kittalabuttiyalli Aralida Akshara Kanasu" ("The alphabet dream that bloomed in Kittalabutti") – the title of one of these news articles – came to be so influential in getting public attention for my efforts. Others began to write about me and publish in different magazines and newspapers.'

'In 2013, I was recognised by Karnataka state. I was able to start a high school. The school was short of teachers. In this, I got help from Veena Jayaschandran. She helped me with recruitment while Hindustan Petroleum (HP) sanctioned 18.6 lakh rupees to construct the buildings for the school.'

All the donors who have contributed to the school are listed on a plaque, but with one exception: Shri Harekala Hajabba himself is not on the list. This is the way he wants it, and explains, 'It is all of them, not me that have achieved this,' when asked why his name isn't on the list.

By 2010, the school had grown and covered every year up to class ten. With increasing public interest and demand from more local families who wished to educate their children, Shri Hajabba secured more funding from donors and a second building was built and completed in June 2012.

Shri Harekala Hajabba, the simple street vendor and son of a fisherman, was finally seeing his dream becoming a reality.

In January 2020, it was announced that Shri Harekala Hajabba was to receive his highest honour yet, being conferred Padma Shri, the fourth-highest civilian award in India in recognition of his years of effort and dedication to bring to reality his dream of a village school.

On the occasion of his investiture by Shri Ram Nath Kovind, President of the Republic of India, before stepping forward to present himself, Shri Hajabba, humble as always, took off his shoes when receiving the award. 'How could a poor man like me wear footwear in front of the Honourable President and all those guests and receive such a prestigious award? I removed my shoes for that reason,' he explained.

Currently, the Hajabba School, as it is known, has 175 students in attendance, drawn from communities living in Newpadupa and surrounding villages. 'A lot of children have been educated in our school right from primary school through to high school level,' Shri Hajabba reflected. 'Some of these children have gone on to become engineers, others have qualified as doctors, and some have become teachers. There are also some of our students who have gone abroad to study and many have gone on to establish careers and become householders, to live and succeed in cities.'

The world we live in is far from perfect, and if we want things to get better, we have to be the ones who decide to make a change, to make the world better. Shri Hajabba by his years of tireless dedication has shown that one does not have to be famous or wealthy to make change. Despite his own difficulties, Shri Hajabba has made a difference in the lives of hundreds of children by identifying problems and being determined to find solutions.

If we want a better world, we need more people like Shri Hajabba. The question now is can there be enough of them and who has the courage to be one like him?

12

For Bharat Mata and Sanatana Dharma: Shri P. Parameswaran

Pradeep Krishnan

Is it not rare to find a prolific writer, unique reformer, first-rate poet, eloquent speaker, astute historian, powerful orator, and shrewd organiser, all rolled into one personality? Yet, such a unique being, an exceptional genius, Sri P. Parameswaran, lived amongst us in Kerala, the land of Adi Shankaracharya, spreading light all around. Born in 1927, his earthly sojourn of ninety-three years was destined to work for one objective: to defend Bharat, *Bharatiya sanskriti* – Indian culture – and Hindu dharma. I am gratified and thankful that a serendipitous meeting with him in 1980 changed the course of my life, offering me the opportunity to have Shri P. Parameswaranji as my guru and to have a close connection and interaction with him until his passing.

I vividly recall that first encounter. I was then an eighteen-year-old brimming with confidence bordering on arrogance, seeming to know about the causes of all societal ills. My socialisation and schooling had convinced me that Communism was the way forward. In my mind, the repressive forces of religion, tradition, and caste were ailing Indian society and had to be uprooted and replaced. Communism would usher in a new world of prosperity, real freedom, workers' rights and social equality.

Parameswaranji listened patiently with a calm and gentle demeanour while I raged on about the evils of Hindu customs and civilisation, describing it as superstitious, regressive, divisive, caste ridden, and outdated.

Unfazed by my tirade, Parameswaranji looked at me with a benign smile and quipped, 'Pradeep, please tell me the texts that you have read to come to this conclusion. Without learning any principal treatise, how can one either understand or criticise?'

At the time, other than repeat what I had read in the communist literature, I had little argument to offer. Thus began my journey of self-discovery seeing at close quarters, the life and work of a remarkable human being.

Through his books, speeches and social reform activities, Parameswaranji, as he was affectionately addressed, dedicated a lifetime to protecting and promoting Indian culture, spirituality, and sanatana dharma, influencing and bringing social consciousness to tens of thousands of people. Rather than imposing his ideas, he inspired countless seekers to delve deep and study *Bharatiya* thought and culture.

Born in a devout Malayali Hindu family in Muhamma, a small village near Alleppey, Kerala, from his childhood days Parameswaranji was immersed in the fundamentals of Hindu traditions and culture, learning to recite scared *shlokas* and *mantras* from his father, a *purohithan* (presiding priest) in a local temple.

A brilliant student, Parameswaranji graduated as a gold medallist BA (Hons) in history. While still a student, Parameswaranji was greatly influenced by two charismatic thinkers: Swami Vivekananda and Guruji Golwalkar, *sarsangachalak* (president) of the Rastriya Swayam Sevak Sangh.

As a schoolboy, Parameswaranji eagerly awaited the receipt of books of Swami Vivekananda through post. Reading Swamiji's *Colombo to Almora* and *To the Youth of India* sparked a deep urge within him to connect to the culture and traditions of India. Also greatly influenced by Swami Agamananda, founder of the Advaita Ashrama at Kalady, the birthplace of Adi Sankara, the young Parameswaran accompanied Swami Agamananda on a pilgrimage to what is today known as Kolkata, to seek blessings and *deeksha* (initiation) from Swami Virajananda at the Belur math. About the encounter with his *Deeksha Guru*, Parameswaranji once recalled, 'Swami Virajananda had a charming personality. He welcomed me with brilliant, piercing eyes and a graceful and affectionate smile as I prostrated before him to receive his blessings. It all remains fresh in my memory. The impact was much more than his physical presence.'

On meeting Guruji, he wrote, 'As we all sat in well-ordered lines facing the platform in front, Sri Guruji, as we affectionately and respectfully called him, stepped into the hall, accompanied by two or three office bearers. All of us stood up, thrilled by the magnetic personality of this charismatic leader. Instantly, we felt that we were in the presence of a powerful personality who held the destiny of the country in his hand. It was a mixture of spiritual power, within one who knew no fear, was full of compassion, and absolutely confident of his mission in life. Though that was the first camp I ever attended, it was a defining moment. We listened to him in rapt attention, answered his questions and came back beaming with a vision of the future Hindu society. The path ahead for me was clear and

I never looked back. I decided to become a Sangh *pracharak* [preacher] on completion of my study.'

And so, the intelligent and idealistic Parameswaran took on social work as a life goal. Soon, recognising the young man's organisational potential, Guruji asked him to be the organising secretary of the Bharatiya Jan Sangh, a political party.

Turning Point

In 1975, the Indira Gandhi government declared a National Emergency. All elections were suspended, leading opposition leaders were jailed, and other fundamental freedom of citizens frozen. Parameswaranji was among the tens of thousands of political opponents arrested up and down the country and found himself jailed for nineteen months. When the National Emergency was lifted in 1977, elections were called and the Janata Party – a conglomerate of several opposition parties – came to power. However, Parameswaranji, noting the lack of principles and craze for power among the new leaders, felt saddened and deeply disappointed by the turn of events.

But Parameswaranji redirected his energies in positive directions. Recognising the importance of social work, he joined the Deendayal Research Institute, a social institution founded by his close friend Nanaji Deshmukh, who himself had earlier quit politics. As Director of the Institute, Parameswaranji not only organised seminars and discussions on topics of cultural and social interest across Indian society but also worked relentlessly at the grassroot level to improve the living conditions of village people, managing several self-help projects such as building schools.

Bharatheeya Vichara Kendram

Seeing the multifaceted challenges which the people of his home state, Kerala, were facing, particularly the dominance and rising political clout of Marxist ideas in the social and political sphere and the detrimental effects they were having on indigenous culture and values, Parameswaranji's inclinations urged him on to set up a forum that fostered intellectual dialogue to counter them. Thus, in 1982, on the auspicious day of Vijayadasami, the Bharatheeya Vichara Kendram (BVK), a centre for national reconstruction through study and research was established with headquarters at Thiruvananthapuram, Kerala. Since then, BVK has been at the forefront in the drive to preserve and nurture the indigenous traditions and cultural ethos of the India that is Bharat.

Parameswaranji's guidance paved the pathway for the Kendram, which conducted research and organised multiple seminars and symposiums on topics of regional and national importance – such as an assessment of the diverse streams engaged in the national freedom movement leading to Independence; the controversy and truth behind the so-called Aryan Invasion; the societal challenges due to the changing face of Kerala; the Uniform Civil Code; the effects of Indira's imposition of the National Emergency in 1975; Kerala Sanskrit Sammelan; Nila Vichara Sathram, a seminar on the ecological and cultural history of Bharathapuzha; Kerala and freedom struggle; and research into strategies for national resurgence.

Ever a consummate communicator, Parameswaranji never imposed on others, only offering options and getting one to think critically. Through his mentorship, members of the Kendram learnt much about effective communication, leadership, negotiation, diplomacy, and handling media.

Thanks to Parameswaranji's organisational acumen and the national importance of the subjects that the Kendram was researching, these events attracted the best of India's intellectuals to contribute. Over the years, BVK has hosted a spectrum of distinguished scholars, thinkers and cultural and social leaders. H.H. the Dalai Lama, Justices Rama Joice, V.R. Krishna Iyer and K.T. Thomas, Swami Ranganathananda, Swami Chinmayananda, K.S. Sudharshan, A.P. Venkateshwaran, L.K. Advani, Dr Murli Manohar Joshi, Arun Shourie, Jag Mohan, Dr M.G.S Narayanan, Dr G. Madhavan Nair, Michel Danino, Francois Goutier, S. Gurumurthy, Dr J.K Bajaj, Dr E.C.G. Sudharsan, Prof. Manoj Das, and Dr V.R Panchamukhi – all participated in these deliberations.

Today, along with thirty-odd units located in different parts of Kerala, the Kendram has grown to become a hive for thinkers and researchers rooted in the cultural and spiritual ethos of Bharat. Through publishing books and organising camps, debates, symposia, and classes over the years, BVK has made important inroads raising cultural awareness within Kerala. It is influential within academic circles and continues to attract a strong constituent of young people, who participate in seminars on history, philosophy, economics, politics, education, environment and ecology, development, society and life, and management.

Parameswaranji was instrumental in helping launch the Swadeshi Science Movement (SSM), which was founded in 1989. SSM is a popular science movement dedicated to the overall development of India by means of science and technology. Later, inspired by SSM, Vijnana Bharati movement was set up with the aim of fostering a harmonious synthesis between the physical and spiritual sciences and cultivating a swadeshi spirit in social progress through science and technology.

In 1996, Parameswaranji became the President of Vivekananda Kendra, originally founded by Eknath Ranade, and remained in this post until his last breath. Talking of Parameswaranji's contributions, Shri A. Balakrishnan, the present President of the kendra, recalls, 'Parameswaranji's presence was a golden period, which stabilised the kendra ship which was rolling in the rough waters. He re-emphasised the vision and mission of Ekanathji Ranade and Swami Vivekananda to kendra workers and made them mentally, intellectually, and spiritually strong to continue the various service activities without interruption.'

Parameswaranji was thus an able successor to Eknath Ranade and during his tenure oversaw the Kendra's dynamic growth in different parts of the country as well as a widening of the range of its activities to several other sectors. Talking of the goal of Vivekananda Kendra, Parameswaranji once said that it was 'to take the message of sanatana dharma as interpreted by Swami Vivekananda to every home, every hamlet, every school, utilising temples and service activities as the media'.

A Versatile Genius

Parameswaranji – well versed in the philosophy of the Vedas, Upanishads and Gita – had followed in detail the thoughts and writings of great Indians and Westerners alike: Swami Vivekananda, Sri Aurobindo, Mahatma Gandhi, Deendayal Upadhyay, Karl Marx, and Arnold Toynbee.

Amidst his busy schedule, Parameswaranji devoted time and energy to writing. During the course of his life, he published around fifty books covering disciplines ranging across philosophy, religion, politics, culture, and society.

Of especial note are these titles: *Sreenarayana Guru: The Prophet of Renaissance*; *Marx and Vivekananda*; *Bhagavad-Gita: Vision of a New World Order*; *Beyond All Isms to Humanism*; *Marxilninnu Maharshiyilekku (From Marx to Maharshi)*; and *Bhaviyude Darsanikan Sri Aurobindo* (Sri Aurobindo, the Future Philosopher).

In addition to his books, Parameswaranji served as editor of several journals: *Manthan, Kesari, Yuva Bharathi, Pragati,* a quarterly research journal, and *Vivekananda Kendra Patrika.* Of all these works, Parameswaranji's biographical studies on the lives of Shri Narayana Guru and Sri Aurobindo remain unequalled for content and quality. In 1998, Vivekananda Kendra brought out a compendium of Parameswaranji's selected articles in three volumes titled *Heart Beats of the Hindu Nation.*

As a gifted multilingual orator, possessing a great command of words and depth of insight, Parameswaranji delivered lectures all over the country and internationally. Whenever and wherever he talked, people thronged to hear him in large numbers. In 1993, to mark the centenary of Swami Vivekananda's address at the World Parliament of Religions held at Chicago, he was invited to speak at the celebrations in the same city.

A natural poet, Parameswaranji wrote inspiring poems in Malayalam, several of which have become *ganageetham* (group songs) During school days, his thought-provoking Malayalam poem on Kolukonda Vembanad (the troubled waters of Vembanad backwaters) had won Parameswaranji the first prize while in competition against his classmate Vayalar Rama Varma, who went on to become a well-known lyricist. During his long career and service in scholastic and social work, Parameswaranji interacted closely with several Malayalam literary figures – such as Akkittam Achutan Namboothiri, Sukumar Azhikode, Dr Ayyappa Panicker,

Vishnu Narayanan Namboothiri, Sugathakumari, and Prof. Guptan Nair – demonstrating his receptiveness to a breadth of ideas and deep connectedness with Malayali roots. Besides scholastic pursuits, Parameswaranji also maintained close contact with spiritual luminaries and institutions such as Mata Amritanandamayi, Swami Ranganathannada and the Sri Ramakrishna Ashram and Sri Aurobindo Ashram.

Social Initiatives

Parameswaranji, clad in a white dhoti, simple cotton shirt and with his forehead always marked with sandalwood *tilak,* was considered a saint in the Kerala social scene. In the eighties, when Marxists unleashed large-scale violence against Sangh cadres, he took initiatives to put an end to the ensuing mindless political violence. His humanistic pleas to engage in ideological debate rather than violence and physical conflict were widely welcomed. This respect for Parameswaranji cut across ideological divides where, even Marxist leaders, otherwise opposed to Parameswaranji, held him in high regard, and Communist leaders of the stature of E.M.S. Namboothiripad, P. Govinda Pillai, and C. Achuta Menon enjoyed a very close relationship with him.

In 1998, as an answer to rising crime, delinquency and other social evils plaguing Kerala, Parameswaranji proposed as a solution the study of Bhagavad Gita as a comprehensive life science. This suggestion, well received by many social and religious leaders, initiated a massive cultural movement with several Gita Swadhyaya Samithees (GSS) – Gita awareness committees – being formed to spread awareness of the Gita across Kerala. Thanks to his insightful initiative, GSS have continued to remain strong, offering formal classes, seminars, and lectures in Gita philosophy with active participation of university students as well as folks from every walk of life.

In December 2000, an international seminar on 'Bhagavad-Gita and modern problems' was held at Thiruvananthapuram at Parameswaranji's initiative. This seminar, inaugurated by H.H. the Dalai Lama, attracted around fifteen hundred young people, and included several scholars, intellectuals, academics, and saints from India and abroad.

Parameswaranji was instrumental in organising the Vishala Hindu Sammelan, which was a call for community unity though the unifying principle of 'Hindus are one'. He infused fresh life into local traditions and customs by instituting the observation of 'Ramayana Month' during Karkadakam, the last month in the Malayali calendar.

Parameswaranji's life was lived in selfless dedication to Mother India and sanatana dharma. Always shunning positions of power, he maintained his commitment to serving society as a *sevak*. He even politely declined a ministerial post in the Atal Bihari Vajpayee government, instead suggesting Shri O. Raja Gopal, a friend and very able person, as the ideal alternative.

Perhaps the most appropriate way of remembering Shri Parameswaranji is to recall Mata Amritanandamayi, who, having closely observed Parameswaranji's selfless lifestyle, once remarked that his life reminded her of Bharata, younger brother of Shri Rama of the Ramayana – living a life of service.

Awards and Recognitions

In 1997, in recognition of his efforts in teaching the principles of Hinduism, Shri Parameswaranji was awarded the Bhaiji Hanuman Prasad Poddar Award instituted by Bada Bazaar Library of Calcutta (Kolkata). In 2000, he was made a member of the Court of Jawaharlal Nehru University, New Delhi. In 2002, he was awarded the Amritha Keerthi Puraskar cultural award by Sri Matha Amrithananda Mayi Mutt for outstanding service to society. His book titled *Disa Bhotathinte Darshanam* won the Kerala Sahitya Akademi Award.

Considering his outstanding services to the society, the nation honoured him with Padma Shri in 2004 and Padma Vibhushan in 2018.

Farewell to the Rishi

A noble life of ninety-three years came to an end on 9 February 2020, at an Ayurvedic hospital in Ottappalam, Palakkad District, when Parameswaranji breathed his last. In a message, Prime Minister Narendra Modi said, 'Shri P Parameswaran was a proud and dedicated son of Bharat Mata. His was a life devoted to India's cultural awakening, spiritual regeneration and serving the poorest of the poor. Parameswaranji's thoughts were prolific, and his writings were outstanding. He was indomitable. An institution builder, he nurtured eminent institutions such as the Bharatheeya Vichara Kendram, Vivekananda Kendra and others. I am fortunate to have interacted with him many times. He was a towering intellectual. Anguished by his demise. Om Shanti.'[1]

Even the Marxist Chief Minister of Kerala, Shri Pinarayi Vijayan, paid his respects and said that P. Parameswaranji was a profound scholar whose life equalled that of a *rishi* – one who dedicated his life to the values he believed in.[2]

I offer this tribute – my guru dakshina – to a legend who four decades ago became my first guru. Parameswaranji paved the way for my transformation from a self-doubting atheist to a sanatani, one who came to know who he was, and the culture and traditions that have forged him and define him.

To quote the words of Sri J. Nandakumar, thinker and national convenor of the intellectual movement Prajna Pravah, 'As the legendary poet, Rabindranath Tagore said: Death is not extinguishing the light; it is only putting out the lamp because the dawn has come. For us, Parameswaranji is an ever-burning lamp, the divine lamp that never ceases to burn. He will continue to be the light on our path as before.'

Notes

Chapter 2: The Hospital That Subhasini Mistry Built

1   Tamaghna Banerjee, 'No One Should Die because they are Poor – Subhasini Mistry', Interview in *The Times of India*, 28 January 2018, https://timesofindia.indiatimes.com/city/kolkata/no-one-should-die-because-they-are-poor-subhasini-mistry/articleshow/62678189.cms (accessed 20 May 2024).
2   Rabi Banerjee, 'The Good Doctor', *The Week*, 9 August 2020, https://www.theweek.in/theweek/statescan/2020/07/30/the-good-doctor.html (accessed 20 May 2024).

Chapter 4: Rekindling Kalaripayattu: A Spotlight on India's Forgotten Heritage

1   200 BCE to 600 CE.
2   Specialised Brahmin-run institutes that produced martially trained Brahmin celibates, *Brahmakashtram* (Warrior Brahmins). Also known as Kalam or Ghatikas.
3   This coincided with the establishment of the Kollamvarsham or the Malayalam era, the death of Adi Shankara, overthrow of the Cholas, and the founding of a new Chera capital in Makotai.
4   This period in Kerala was marked by a complex decentralised system of governance that was 'multiplex and contestatory'. Four major powers existed. In the north, Kolachiris of Kolathunatu and Zamorins of Kozhikode in what could be arbitrarily labelled as Madhya-Kerala, the ruler of Kochi held sway and the Raja of Travancore in the south was the reigning authority. Each of these states or kingdoms was subdivided into various districts known as *nadu*, which, in turn, were further divided into counties referred to as *desams*. Within the *desams* were numerous villages called *amsa*. At the helm of each district was a *nadu vali*, who possessed the authority to preside over both criminal and civil matters.

The next tier of authority comprised the *desa vali*, responsible for overseeing the maintenance and training of local Kalari establishments.

5   These ballads are of two kinds, the *Puthooram Pattukal warriors* and the *Thacholi Pattukal*, concerning Theyyaa/Ezhavaa and Nair/Nayyars *Chevakas* (military servicemen), respectively. The Nayyars, although considered to be of Shudra origin, went to form multiple royal lineages in the region and served as functionaries at all levels of society. Legend says that the Ezhavas are descendants of martial warriors from Elam (Sri Lanka) sent by the King at the request of the Chera king as far back as the 1st century CE. Another origin story considers them as progeny of *Villavar* (bowmen) from Tulu Nadu. A third prominent group known as Cattars (or Yatra) were prominent Kalari experts. Cattars were essentially *Brahmkshatra* lineages who had not given up the martial practices.

6   Theyyam is a ritualistic dance of northern Kerala. Theyyam is heavily influenced by Kalaripayattu with the dance involving the Kalari body movements. Legends of Kalaripayattu have also been deified in Theyyam dances. Heroes like Othenan, Mannappan and Kathirur Gurukkal have been elevated as Gods.

7   In popular culture, Pazhassi Raja is acknowledged as South India's inaugural freedom fighter.

8   Meenakshi Amma will play the lead role in a multilingual film titled *Look Back*. The movie is helmed by Rajan Mullaratt under the banner of Kalari Gurukulam, Bengaluru.

9   Kalaripayattu was taught only during the monsoon season, June to September.

Chapter 6: A Tongue on Every Stone: The Life of K.K. Muhammed

1   K.K. Muhammed refers to this in his autobiography, *An Indian I am*, Prabhat Prakashan, New Delhi, 2023, p. 81.

2   https://timesofindia.indiatimes.com/india/ram-temple-existed-before-babri-mosque-in-ayodhya-archaeologist-kk-muhammed/articleshow/71391712.cms (accessed 20 May 2024).

Chapter 12: For Bharat Mata and Sanatana Dharma: Shri P. Parameswaran

1   https://www.narendramodi.in/prime-minister-narendra-modi-pm-condoles-demise-of-p-parameswaran-548349   (accessed 20 May 2024). Taken from his Tweets published on 9 February 2020.

2   Pinarayi Vijayan's quote: Parameswaran: https://organiser. org/2020/02/17/126637/bharat/2_02_21_02_a_1/   (accessed 20 May 2024).

Glossary

abhanga	Hindu devotional song and music, compare to *bhajan*
acharya	A Hindu spiritual teacher and mentor
Amma	Mother
anubhava	Insight, experience, experiential
atman	That which is the eternal core of one's being that transmigrates or attains release upon death
BAIF	Bhartiya Agro Industries Foundation
baithak or baithaks	Meeting, conversation, conference
bhajan	Hindu devotional song and music; compare *abhanga*
Bharatiya	Indigenous; Indian
chajja	Balcony
dacoity	Robbery, sometimes accompanied by violence
Devi Parayanam	Incantation of all the Devis' names
dhanam	Donation to some religious or other good cause
dharma	In Hindu philosophy, this is the inherent nature of reality, that which is in accord with custom, preserves order through right conduct, and way of living

ganageetham or *ganageethams*	Song, often Hindu devotional, often sung in a group; see also *bhajan*
gumate	A traditional clay-pot-shaped percussion instrument with a leather skin
Halakki *Vokkaliga*	A Vanvasi community of Uttar Kannada to which Sukri Bommagowda belongs
haldi kumkum *ceremony*	Hindu social gathering where married women exchange haldi (turmeric) and kumkum (vermillion) which symbolise their married status and wishing long lives for their husbands
kattaata	A folk game
krithi	Carnatic musical composition, usually Hindu religious
kuladaivam	Family or clan deity, usually with a dedicated shrine
lakh	One hundred thousand
lakshana	A quality, characteristic, or auspicious mark
mamta	Motherly love; nurturing love
mani	In the context of Halakki culture, beads used in jewellery
maanyata	Lit. ideas and customs that are accepted and used in daily living; recognition of skills or value of work
mahila *adyaksh*	Woman chair on a local committee
maryaada	Lit. dignified, controlled, and calm; one who follows their dharma
mathas	Also, *mutt, mutth* – Hindu institute or college usually affiliated with a Hindu temple

moringa	Drumstick tree, whose pods are so shaped and have anti-inflammatory properties eaten widely across India
nagli	Finger millet
nirukt	Etymology: that which is uttered, pronounced, or explained
NITI Aayog	National Institute for Transforming India – a government of India organisation
pagade	A cross and circle game played on a board made of wood or cloth and either shells or four-sided long dice, also called *chaupar* in other parts of India
parampara	Traditions associated with a specific lineage of Hindu, Buddhist or Jain teachers/gurus
parivrjaka	A renunciate
pracharak	Someone appointed to promote a cause via personal contact, meetings, and lectures
pravachana	An oral discourse, exposition, or explanation of spiritual concepts in the Hindu tradition
pind	Dough balls made especially as offerings at funerals
purohithan	In Hindu tradition, a priest who presides over devotional ritual in temple or offers guidance
rishi	Hindu seer/sage accomplished in Vedic texts; revealler of divine knowledge
sadhana	Means by which spiritual enlightenment is achieved in Hindu dharma

salai	Specialised Brahmin run institutes that produced martially trained Brahmin celibates, *Brahmakashtram* (Warrior Brahmins). Also known as Kalam or Ghatikas.
sanyasin	A renunciate, one who having attained the fourth and last stage, will not be reborn and whose atman will be absorbed into the universal, divine, oneness
sarsangachalak	Head of a sangha; designation used for the head of Rashtriya Swayamsevak Sangh
sastanga pranam	Prostration, showing deep respect
satyagraha	Lit. *satya* = truth and *agraha* = insistence, so insistence upon truth; a term for nonviolent resistance
seva	Service or offering, often associated with Hindu religiously motivated work, deed, or worship
sevak	One who offers seva – see *seva*
shakti	Divine energy personified in the feminine form
shishta	Goodness; cultured and learned; to speak grammatically correctly
shishya	A student, a disciple, a seeker, associated with a guru in the role of mentor, teacher
shukravaaraa	Lit. Sanskrit word for Friday, with variant, Sukri as a feminine name
suggi	A type of folk dance in Uttara Kannada
taluka	An administrative unit within a district consisting of several villages

thala	A place, in respect of Kalari
Tulsi Puja	Also known as *Tulsi Vivah*, a Hindu ceremony marking the marriage of Tulsi with Shri Vishnu
vanvasi	A forest dwelling community
varai	Barnyard millet
vibhuti	Lit. an incarnation of Brahman or divine power

About the Curator and Contributors

 **Jay Jina** is the director of Chitraayana, a vertical within INDICA. He has edited and co-authored a series of three books on India's cultural heritage. This volume is the fourth in the series (the most recent being *Anveshana*). Before this project, Jay mentored young writers on a creative writing programme. Being from an applied mathematics background, most of Jay's professional career has been in industries such as automotive, aerospace, and instrumentation where he held several senior-level positions predominantly in the areas of manufacturing, logistics, strategy, and information systems. This industry career was interspersed with periods in academia and consultancy with the Big Four. For several years, Jay taught executive MBA programmes. Apart from his role within INDICA, Jay teaches mathematics in a UK university. Jay was born in Africa to Indian descent parents. He now lives in the UK.

Madhavi Girish Kunte holds an M.Sc. in medical microbiology, an MBA in marketing, and a PG diploma in intellectual property rights. In the past, she worked as a marketing executive for a stem cell banking company and as a patent analyst for an intellectual property firm.

Besides the essay in this collection, Madhavi has co-authored three other anthologies for INDICA, the manuscripts of which are currently in the publication process.

Reading and narrating stories across genres has been Madhavi's hobby ever since she can remember. Madhavi is currently working on her first novel, set in the contemporary world, and pursuing the path of a full-time storyteller, writing stories in the genres of myths and contemporary fiction.

Madhavi is based out of Bangalore, where she gets to be a happy, stay-at-home mother of two adorable children aged 8 and 5 years.

Santhini Govindan is a writer, primarily of children's literature, having written picture books and concept books for young children, feature and chapter books for middle-grade readers, and stories for young adults. She has more than fifty published books for children. Stories and poems that she has written are widely used in more than one hundred English readers and school textbooks across India, the Middle East, and South Asia. Her first stand-alone poetry book – a collection of original poetry for children, *To Catch a Poem*, which has over one hundred poems in different rhyme schemes – was published in March 2022 by Ukiyoto Publications. Santhini has won numerous awards for her work and has been awarded two fellowships by the Government of India for projects connected to children's literature in India. She has conducted creative writing workshops at schools across India and has taught creative writing at the undergraduate level at the Mumbai University.

Santhini lives in Mumbai with her husband. She has a son, a daughter, and four grandchildren, whom she likes to indulge. Apart from reading and writing, she enjoys working on embroidery and crochet projects, gardening, and playing with pets. She is an inveterate collector of bells and angels, and her burgeoning collection threatens to overrun her home!

Mythili Rao earned her PhD in Hindi literature from Bangalore University. Until September 2023, she served the Jain Group of Institutions in various positions, enjoying a fruitful 27-year career in teaching and administration. During her time in academia, having developed an interest in Gandhian thought and principles, Mythili offered an elective paper 'Gandhian Thought and Literary Responses' to undergraduate students across disciplines.

Apart from participating and presenting papers in national and international conferences throughout her career, Mythili has also chaired sessions, given keynote address, and been chief guest in about 60 events. Engaging with fellow academics widely, she has travelled to various countries including Austria, Belgium, and Japan.

Mythili has received awards from organisations in recognition for her contributions to Hindi and has served as an advisor and consultant on various government committees and university boards. Her literary competency in English and Kannada has over a period of time enabled Mythili to develop an interest in translation studies. She is currently engaged in the translation of literary texts from Kannada to Hindi and is a member of the NCERT Curricular Area Group for Hindi.

Patañjali Pundit is an entrepreneur, a freelance writer, a historian by training, and a wannabe polyglot. He graduated in political science and history from St. Stephen's College, Delhi University, and holds a dual master's degree in international and global history from Columbia University and the London School of Economics. Pundit's academic focus has been primarily on ancient Indian history and international relations. Guided by his study of classical Sanskrit texts, his preoccupations span the realms of Indian mythology and philosophical traditions.

Patañjali blends scholarly research with vivid storytelling to weave narratives that bridge the gap between tradition and modernity. His writings reflect a deep understanding of history, politics, and culture interwoven with personal experiences. Through his exploration of ancient Indian history and philosophy, Patañjali seeks to unravel the complexities of contemporary global affairs, examining how cultural and civilisational values shape political systems and international relations.

In his free time, he can be found devouring science fiction-fantasy novels at cafés in Delhi or summiting peaks in some remote part of the world.

Munmun Banerjee is an engineer from Bangalore. She has a master's degree in computer applications from NIT, Raipur, and her professional journey in information technology has always been intertwined with a passion for exploring the vast and varied landscapes of culture, especially that of her rich Indian heritage.

While working in Europe, she often came across misconceptions and biases concerning India, which motivated her to delve into a deeper understanding of the culture and traditions of her roots.

Beyond her professional and exploratory endeavours, Munmun cherishes her role as a mother to an 8-year-old. Through her tales of adventure and discovery, she hopes to instil in him a deep appreciation for India's rich heritage and the importance of breaking stereotypes.

Ramanujam S.R. is a traveller with fascination for heritage and the hills. His professional work in infrastructure development has taken him to many corners and hinterland of India. This gradually created an urge to learn about India's heritage and temple architecture and to experience the devotion – *bhakti* – that created them. Discussions with friends helped him explore and discover places unimagined before. Together they read about their shared rich cultural history and began to create and share regular quizzes on Indian heritage under the banner IndiYatra (IndiYatra.in). These quizzes cover Indian history, heritage, and culture and are released on festival days. He is currently writing a book in the Chitraayana series for INDICA on the Temples of Himachal Pradesh from the viewpoint of a pilgrim.

Ramanujam lives in Mumbai with his wife Rajashree. She shares his enthusiasm for Indian culture and heritage and has encouraged him to travel and discover Indian heritage. Their children, Anagha and Gopal, are college students, and both parents hope that the culture bug passes on to them as well.

Avatans Kumar is a linguist and columnist. He graduated in linguistics from Jawaharlal Nehru University, New Delhi, where he was also an MPhil scholar and taught undergraduate courses in linguistics.

Avatans then joined the graduate programme in linguistics at the University of Illinois at Urbana-Champaign. As a researcher, Avatans taught Hindi as a foreign language and received the Henry R. Kahane Award for Outstanding Teaching Assistant in non-Western languages. Avatans has attended Bharatiya Vidya Bhavan's journalism programme, holds an MBA, and has worked in information technology in the financial sector for several years.

Avatans frequently writes about Indian knowledge tradition, language and culture, and current affairs. His articles have been published by the *Times of India, Sunday*

Guardian, *The Print*, *India Currents*, *DailyO*, and Brownstone Institute. Besides having his own Hindi poems published, Avatans has translated former Indian diplomat Arun Kumar Sahu's original English poetry collection *Iguana and Other Poems* into Hindi – *Iguana aur Anya Kavitayein*. He has recently curated an anthology of short stories – *Flight of Deities: An Anthology of Desecration and Devotion* (2023) – published by Notion Press. Avatans received the San Francisco Press Club's Journalism Award in 2021, 2022, and 2023.

Avatans lives in the USA, where his community involvement includes teaching Hindi and dharma to diaspora children at the local *mandir* or temple. He was also head coach and ran the sports programme as the athletic director at his daughter's school. As trustee, Avatans also leads the US operations of Indic Academy, incorporated as INDICA, Inc., a not-for-profit organisation. INDICA seeks to preserve India's traditional institutions, knowledge, and practices, protect her identity against distortions, and promote Indic thought to local and global consumers, practitioners, and seekers.

Aparna M. Sridhar is a career journalist and is currently Chief Editor, Conversations, INDICA. She has also worked with INDICA's Centre for Soft Power, showcasing India's attractions to the world. Having deep roots in the Thanjavur region of Tamil Nadu, once the hub of Indian art and culture, she edited India's only exclusively Indian classical music magazine *Samagana: The First Melody* for five years.

In 2023, Aparna's research paper 'Broadening AI Ethics Narratives: An Indic Art View' was published at the ACM Conference on Fairness, Accountability and Transparency held in Chicago.

Aparna is married, and she and her husband have two children and a pet Labrador.

Aniya Burse is fourteen and lives in the USA with her parents and younger brother.

Besides writing, Aniya enjoys playing flute, chess, and reading fantasy and sci-fi novels. Her fourth-grade teacher introduced her to creative writing through an assignment she particularly enjoyed. Aniya recalls that the premise of the assignment was based on Zathura, the sequel to the popular book *Jumanji*.

However, Aniya truly began to write at age eleven amidst the COVID-19 pandemic when her mother enrolled her in writing classes to help kill her chronic boredom. Much to her mother's surprise, Aniya fell in love writing.

Aniya is obsessed with writing fiction, and so far, her writing has been published in seven anthologies: five short stories and two poems. This meant that non-fiction was put on the back burner until this project. Aniya is excited to have her first biographical essay published in this Padma Anthology through INDICA.

After high school, Aniya plans to go to medical school and become a doctor, and continue with writing.

Ishaan Channa Reddy is fourteen and lives in the USA. He was born to Indian parents, who have instilled in him the values of hard work and honesty.

Ishaan became interested in writing at a young age, creating various fictional characters. When he got word of the opportunity to tell the story of a Padma Shri awardee, he thought it would be a good way to share his writing and get mentoring, guidance, and professional feedback through which he could develop his writing skills.

After high school, Ishaan plans to go to college, become a lawyer, and write books.

Pradeep Krishnan was born in 1962 in Thodupuzha, Kerala, in a traditional Hindu family. During college years, the influence of student politics led his thinking towards Marxism, and for some time, he held the view that the ideal of an egalitarian society made it imperative to not only ridicule but do away with God, gurus, rituals, customs, and traditions.

After graduating in commerce and law and completing a post graduate diploma in journalism, Pradeep served the central government for 36 years. A serendipitous meeting in 1980 with the late Sri P. Parameshwaran, then a senior RSS pracharak, paved the way for Pradeep's transformation into a devout and spiritual seeker, and being committed to progress and betterment of society through independent thought, indigenous knowledge, and Indic values.

A voracious reader and itinerant traveller, Pradeep has over the past four decades spent extended periods discovering the amazing diversity and unity of India first-hand. Travelling from Kutch to Kamrup and stretching from Kanyakumari to Kashmir, he has spent much time visiting sacred places and interacting with countless lay folk and gurus alike.

He is a passionate writer, and for the past several years, he has contributed articles to several periodicals and online portals in English, Hindi, and Malayalam. Among his works are 50 published interviews with several eminent persons.

Pradeep lives with his wife, Sreelakshmi, in Thiruvananthapuram, Kerala.